5 MINUTES
TO JUMPSTARTING YOUR REAL ESTATE CAREER

John D. Mayfield

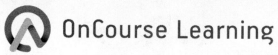

5 Minutes to Jumpstarting Your Real Estate Career

John D. Mayfield

Executive Editor: Sara Glassmeyer

Project Manager: Arlin Kauffman, LEAP Publishing Services

Print and Digital Project Manager: Abigail Franklin

Art and Cover Composition: Chris Dailey

Cover Image: © Shutterstock / Volodymyr Kyrylyuk

Chapter Opener Images:

Chapter 1: © Shutterstock
Chapter 2: © Shutterstock / Brian A. Jackson
Chapter 3: © Shutterstock
Chapter 4: © Shutterstock / Gajus
Chapter 5: © Shutterstock / Vitalliy
Chapter 6: © Shutterstock
Chapter 7: © Shutterstock
Chapter 8: © Shutterstock
Chapter 9: © Shutterstock
Chapter 10: © Shutterstock / Elena Elisseeva
Chapter 11: © Shutterstock / Peteri
Chapter 12: © Shutterstock / Michael Vines
Chapter 13: © Shutterstock
Chapter 14: © Shutterstock
Chapter 15: © Shutterstock
Chapter 16: © Shutterstock / izzet ugutmen

© 2015 OnCourse Learning

ALL RIGHTS RESERVED. No part of this work covered by the copyright herein may be reproduced, transmitted, stored, or used in any form or by any means graphic, electronic, or mechanical, including but not limited to photocopying, recording, scanning, digitizing, taping, web distribution, information networks, or information storage and retrieval systems, except as permitted under Section 107 or 108 of the 1976 United States Copyright Act, without the prior written permission of the publisher.

> For product information and technology assistance, contact us at
> **OnCourse Learning Sales Support, 1-855-733-7239.**
>
> For permission to use material from this text or product.

Library of Congress Control Number: 2015914861

ISBN-13: 978-1-62980-022-6

ISBN-10: 1-62980-022-8

OnCourse Learning
3100 Cumberland Blvd., Suite 1450
Atlanta, GA 30339
USA

Visit us at **www.oncoursepublishing.com**

Dedication

This book is dedicated to my good real estate friend, Kirkor Ajderhanyan. Kirkor and his entire family (Karine, Garen, Teni, Nareg and of course the grandchildren) have been a true blessing to me and my wife. I appreciate and value your friendship more than words could ever say. Thank you for allowing me to be a part of the French Real Estate Industry, and to help at Agency 107 Promenade in Nice, France, my home away from home.

Thank you to Abby Franklin, Molly Armstrong-Paschal, and Lisa Beasley for their helpful editing and excellent suggestions to improve the manuscript. Thanks also to Brian Sholly with OnCourse Learning, and a special thanks to Sara Glassmeyer, my editor. Sara has assisted and guided me since my very first book in 2003. Not many authors can claim such a long and successful working relationship with the same editor over such a long time span. I appreciate all your support and help, Sara!

I also want to say thank you to my lovely wife, Kerry. You are my best friend, and your support and inspiration is unbelievable and is shown in so many ways! Thank you sweetheart for allowing me to pursue my dreams, and for always being there when I need a helping hand.

Thank you to my two daughters, Allie and Anne. I am so proud of both of you! And thanks, Mom, for introducing me to the field of real estate. Little did I know that my life's passion was hidden in this career I cherish so much.

Contents

FOREWORD		vi
INTRODUCTION		vii
1	Developing a Business Plan for Today's Real Estate Agent	1
2	What is Your Brand?	17
3	Create a Niche to Help Build Your Brand	27
4	Systems and Checklists to Operate Your Business Efficiently	33
5	Organization and Filing for the Real Estate Professional	37
6	Presentations with Pizzazz	45
7	Introduction to Prospecting	57
8	Your Secret Tool, Your Sphere of Influence	63
9	Developing a Referral Network That Pays Big Dividends	79
10	Working For-Sale-By-Owners (FSBO's)	91
11	The Secret to Working Expired Listings	101
12	Farming a Geographical Area	113
13	Open Houses that Win Business	129
14	Direct Mail – Today's Hidden Marketing Gem	137

15 Online Marketing Strategies for Your Real Estate Business — 143

16 Why Accountability Matters — 155

EPILOGUE 163

Foreword

The comprehensive range of this book, time-tested techniques, and authoritative guidance from the author make it an indispensable resource.

John Mayfield offers practical, experienced-based strategies and techniques for managing virtually every aspect of your real estate career. Drawing on his first-hand knowledge, it provides practical guidelines, critical information and comprehensive strategies for real estate professionals.

I have had the privilege of knowing and working with John for more than a decade. These experiences allow me to objectively comment on his personal qualities and professional acumen. His contributions and leadership have been instrumental in inspiring tangible changes to our organization as well as the broader real estate community.

John has given of both his time and talents to contribute and lead at both the volunteer level and as a real estate educator. He brings an innovative approach to working with all types of real estate professionals, giving them tools to create and improve their productivity and profitability.

His professional integrity and commitment to give back to the industry are admirable in a climate where time is a scarce resource. I am proud to call John a colleague and friend, but perhaps our greatest reward is having an individual with his résumé of experience, integrity, and leadership as a CRB designee and past president of this organization.

Ginny Shipe, CAE
Real Estate Business Institute (REBI)

Introduction

Welcome to *5 Minutes to Jumpstarting Your Real Estate Career!* Perhaps you purchased this book to help you discover some new ways to get your real estate career off to a great start. Others may be looking for new solutions to help get their businesses out of a rut, and help move their careers to the next level. Whatever your goal, I know you've made the right decision.

I believe that anyone can jumpstart his or her real estate career at whatever level he or she resides. If you're new to the business, you can get off to a great start by following a few simple rules outlined in this book. If you have been in the business for some time and feel as though you need to go to the next level, it's doable! But you must commit to following a few simple rules and guidelines in this book. If you are serious about making a change to your business, or you are committed to getting your career headed in the right direction, I know without a doubt you can easily jumpstart your real estate career with the principles found in this book.

As a real estate broker, author, educational trainer, and graduate with a Master's in Real Estate, I have witnessed firsthand what successful real estate agents do to create business. I am also fortunate to have a successful sales career in the real estate industry. I received my real estate license at the age of eighteen. I started in sales, and I slowly moved my way up into a management position. Eventually, my business grew; I owned three brokerage offices and managed numerous sales agents and assisted them with their careers.

I have trained extensively for several state REALTOR® Associations while assisting these organizations with their Graduate REALTOR® (GRI) programs. GRI is an all-embracing training program for real estate professionals who want to further their educational experience in real estate.

I have also taught and continue to teach for the Council of Real Estate Brokerage Managers (CRB), and I speak and consult with numerous real estate companies around the world regarding their training needs. I have found with my various credentials, extensive practice and observation of some of the most prosperous agents in the field of real estate that I have achieved an integral understanding of what it takes for an agent to become successful in this industry.

In many ways, I have spent countless hours in the so-called "real estate laboratory" (as it has been coined by professionals within the trade), watching other agents perform various tasks. This experience and knowledge has helped me understand what activities and marketing strategies tend to carry the most weight for victory.

Some of the tactics I have incorporated in this "real estate laboratory" have been successful while others did not provide much assistance at all. I will make certain you learn what works, and where you should focus your attention and activities to achieve the greatest results.

I wrote this book to include it in the 5 Minutes series of real estate books currently available. Many of my previous books revolve around marketing and communication. I have also created a book about advertising, sales meetings, and my favorite part of the business, technology. You can discover more information about my previous books at the OnCourse Learning website, (www.oncoursepublishing.com) or from my website, www.businesstechguy.com.

5 Minutes to Jumpstarting Your Real Estate Career can be utilized as a how-to manual for new real estate agents, and for existing or experienced agents. This book is a guide that will help you move your career to the next level. For both the new and experienced agent, this manual can be viewed as a tool for those who need a little coaching in their business lives.

This book is a collection of ideas and resources I believe will help you become successful as a real estate professional. The book is intended to sound like a converstion between you (the student) and me (the coach) so that I can share suggestions, ideas, and strategies I have observed and practiced over the years that can help improve your chances of being successful as a real estate professional.

Again, I have coached and trained hundreds of real estate agents throughout my real estate career, and I do consider myself an optimistic, encouraging teacher. I always convey to others that they can become successful real estate professionals with the right practice and knowledge! However, it is not an easy task to achieve success in real estate sales. You must be willing to work hard, be faithful to your plan, and remind yourself that it will require hard work, dedication and consistency to prevail.

Remember, you must be willing to put in the necessary time and work to reap the rewards. I like to use a garden analogy for building a successful real estate career. For success, you must fertilize, plant the seeds, till the soil, water, cultivate, pull a few weeds, and much more to reach your goals. Don't worry; the result of your labor will be a lush, beautiful garden, the envy of all your neighbors (other real estate agents in your marketplace).

It is also important for you to realize that just because you implement or add one of the suggested marketing ideas included in the upcoming chapters, does not mean money will automatically flow into your bank account. In fact, don't misconstrue the title or believe that you only have to do five minutes of work to witness new money showing up in your life. It will take longer than five minutes or even five days to witness your garden beginning to mature. But over time, and with the proper work and care, I know you will jumpstart your real estate career, regardless of where the professional level is that you currently reside.

As a real estate broker and manager, and a pre-license instructor for a big part of my career, I have witnessed many sales agents come out of the gate selling a big piece of property with little or no effort. They knew a family member, had a friend, or just accidentally walked into a quick and easy sale. Unfortunately, the biggest majority of those folks who had this type of experience also left the real estate business rather quickly. Not everyone understands or realizes that building a successful real estate business relies more on time and patience and less on luck.

After obtaining a great deal of professional and personal research in the real estate industry, I would like to share with you some interesting information from my research, surveys and studies. This introductory chapter will provide you with some excerpts from my findings.

Today's Real Estate Professional

Do real estate agents make enough money to support their monthly business activities? According to the *National Association of REALTORS® 2014 Member Profile*, forty-one percent of sales agents surveyed had a gross income less than $24,999.

This is not positive news for the real estate industry, especially when you consider the median income against a quick and conservative pro-forma statement. The thought that you must consider before broaching a new career, such as real estate, is this: can you make a good return on your investment (R.O.I.) as a real estate professional? The answer is yes, but without the proper mindset, preparation, and determination to have a strong work ethic going in, the results can sometimes seem grim. Table 1 illustrates a sample family budget a typical real estate agent might have.

Table 1 *Sample Monthly Budget*

Monthly Expense Description	Amount
Rent / Mortgage	$1,429.00
Utilities	$250.00
Healthcare	$302.58
Personal Insurance	$460.67
Food	$550.17
Transportation	$750.33
Clothing	$133.67
Entertainment – Dining	$206.83
All Other Expenditures	$460.67
Mobile Phone	$148.00
Office expenses	$546.67*
Total Expenses	**$5,238.62 per month × 12 = $62,863.44**

Note All figures from the Bureau of Labor Statistics, 2013 Consumer Expenditure Survey. (www.bis.gov).
*Median amount for office expenses based on data from the *2014 Member Profile Report*. (National Association of REALTORS, 2014, p. 44).

From this sample family budget, and my research, over fifty percent of the members (sales agents) of the National Association of REALTORS® do not make enough money to break-even each month.

Real estate can be a lucrative career. All of you who are reading this probably know at least one or more successful real estate agents or brokers. However, with the loss of agents in the industry, and because there are so many real estate agents unable to survive financially, I believe there is a need to research and determine what makes some real estate agents more successful than others. It is also important to discover if there are any specific sales and marketing strategies that should be mirrored to gain the greatest return on one's investment as a real estate professional. Addressing these concerns (and others) may provide insights as to what specific marketing activities generate the best results for top-producing real estate agents. It may also help uncover the secrets to "jumpstarting" your real estate career!

Today's Real Estate Consumer

Some of the information collected from *The National Association of REALTORS®* (NAR) 2014 study regarding buyers and sellers, including the characteristics, demographics of buyers and sellers, reasons for buying and selling, and other statistics about the home buying and selling process are shown below:

- The average home buyer is forty-two years old

- First-time home buyers make up thirty-three percent of all buyers

- The typical first-time home buyer is thirty-one years of age

- The repeat buyer's average age is fifty-three years old

- Sixty-five percent of home buyers are married

- Selling a home that is too small is still the primary reason most sellers list their home. This is followed by job relocation, and a desire to be closer to friends and family.

- The typical seller lives in his or her home for ten years, a continuing trend upward from years past.

- Seven in ten sellers only speak to one agent before selecting an agent to work for them

- The longer a home is on the market for sale, the more incentives sellers will offer buyers to consider their property

Included in the information compiled in the NAR 2014 study is how consumers look for homes. I have highlighted the information below in a bulleted list for your reference:

- Eighty-eight percent of buyers use the Internet in some form to search for properties

- Internet users tend to take approximately ten weeks to search for homes

- Eighty-three percent of buyers indicate that photos

- Seventy-nine percent indicated that detailed information is helpful when looking for properties online

- Approximately four out of ten buyers rate virtual tours as helpful. Forty-one percent indicate that interactive maps are useful in property searches.

- Fifty-two percent of buyers indicate that they searched using an iPhone, forty-six percent with an iPad

- Twenty-seven percent of buyers searched with an Android phone

By knowing a few specific characteristics of sales agents, and understanding the demographics and shopping behaviors of consumers, it would seem evident that teaching real estate agents the proper marketing activities to implement would raise their level of income. This might also help prohibit a high exit rate from the real estate industry.

This book will share many prospecting ideas and strategies you can employ to help jumpstart your real estate career. In future chapters, we will focus on marketing tactics you might employ, such as working your sphere of influence, and calling about expired listings and for-sale-by-owner properties. You will also find ideas for developing a business plan, creating your online marketing strategies and more.

I would encourage you to read through all of the ideas and highlight the ones that are of interest to you. Once you've finished with the book, come back to the appropriate section and read through it again, mapping out your game plan.

Take your time reading, enjoy the book, and remember, you're only five minutes away from jumpstarting your real estate career!

Chapter 1

Developing a Business Plan for
Today's Real Estate Agent

Why Working Smart Matters

Okay, now that we're through with the facts, figures, demographics and statistics, let's talk about you, and how you can succeed as a real estate professional. Even if you're an "old timer," wanting to move your career to the next level, what needs to change?

First, you need to learn to work smarter! This book will provide you with a game plan and the tools to work on the right stuff.

Second, speaking of a game plan, you definitely need some type of business plan or strategy to jumpstart your real estate career. You cannot succeed if you are simply throwing darts at a moving target blindfolded. In essence, that is exactly what you are doing if you do not have a game plan.

You also need a positive attitude, and confidence in yourself as a real estate professional. Granted, it's difficult for new agents to muster up confidence in the early stages of a real estate career, but remember, you took the required education, passed the exam and, yes, you are the expert!

Finally, you have to be willing to work hard! Developing (and maintaining) a successful real estate career is not going to be easy. The suggestions, ideas and marketing strategies shared in this book will require tough work, persistence and, yes, more work. Remember, if this were easy, everyone would have a real estate license!

I'm reminded of teaching pre-license real estate classes in St. Louis, Missouri years ago. I would hear some of my students discussing their desire to purchase and drive a BMW, working only weekends–thanks to their future careers in real estate. Sorry to burst your bubble, but it does not always work that way. Successful real estate agents work hard, and the time involved requires much more than only working weekends.

I hope I am not throwing cold water on you, or raining on your parade, but I do want you to know that jumpstarting your real estate career will require:

- Careful planning

- Confidence in yourself as a real estate professional

- Hard work

- Determination

- Persistence

With that said, you can achieve success as a real estate agent, and you can begin this jumpstarting mindset in the next five minutes.

Creating Your Business Plan

With the combination of assets we have discussed, we have the ability to compile an overall profile in our minds of one of today's successful real estate agents: determined, focused, willing to put in long hours to get the job done, a good communicator, and a good listener. Being a good communicator with your clients and other real estate professionals in the field, as well as being a good listener with your mentors and your clients will provide you with an extra foothold as you climb the ladder to your success as a real estate professional.

The background that a successful real estate professional has is much less important than his or her aspirations and willingness to pull up their sleeves and put some dedicated work into the finished product of a successful business. Many successful real estate agents come with many different backgrounds, such as homemaking, teaching, business professions, and an array of other backgrounds. With the right marketing approach, the right mindset, and a focused determination to succeed, you will be on the right track to success. Still, the first step to moving toward your goals as a real estate professional is a plan.

Before we begin discussing your business plan, please know that this book is not a comprehensive manuscript for business planning for the real estate professional. Rather, it is a how-to guide for implementing marketing and sales, prospecting, utilizing technology resources, and gathering various ideas to help you jumpstart your real estate career. Nevertheless, you need to know some specific points and facts to consider when building your business plan. Let's consider some of the following questions when building your business plan.

- What are your strengths as a real estate professional?

- What weaknesses do you possess?

- If you could list some new opportunities for real estate professionals in your marketplace right now or in the next twelve to twenty-four months, what would they be?

- List any threats that you see on the horizon that may be facing the real estate industry or your local marketplace in general.

The four points above are typically used in what is called a S.W.O.T analysis. The following illustration is a good way for you to look at a S.W.O.T. analysis from a chart perspective.

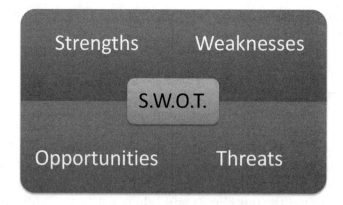

You can create a SWOT analysis on your own, and insert your answers in each one of the appropriate boxes. Please know that your business plan requires much more than a simple S.W.O.T. analysis; however, this is a good place to begin your business planning.

Other questions you may want to consider during your business planning are:

- Who is your competition?

- What are some of the things your competition is doing that you believe you can do better?

- Do you see some weaknesses in your competitive marketplace?

- What is your company's mission statement?

- Do your core values align with the company's core values?

- Speaking of core values, what are the core values you possess as an individual?

- Where would you like to be in five years?

- Where would you like to be in ten years?

- Have you prepared a vision statement? If not, spend a few moments writing out where you would like to be in the next five or ten years. Keep in mind that many individuals like to do this for one year, two years, three years, and or more when creating a plan. Some individuals even write their vision statements, as though they have already achieved their goals and dreams. Any of these options are fine to use.

- What are some ways you can market your real estate business in the next twelve months?

- What are some marketing activities you would like to implement for your real estate career?

- Have you created a personal logo for your real estate business?

- Do you have a tagline or slogan that you might consider using for your real estate career?

These questions and many more are part of developing an effective business plan. The problem for the real estate industry, in general, is that most real estate agents do not have an effective business plan in place. Remember, don't try to throw darts blindfolded at a moving target. Have a business plan! As one of my favorite motivational speakers from the past (Zig Ziglar) would often say, *"You can't hit a target you cannot see and you cannot see a target you do not have."*

Your Business Plan

I believe one reason most real estate agents do so poorly in real estate is because they have no business plan. Without a business plan, you have no direction for your business. It's unfortunate that brokers and managers fail to place more emphasis on the mechanics and reasons for establishing and executing a business plan when new real estate agents come on board. Borrowing another famous quote from Zig Ziglar, *"If you aim at nothing, you will hit it every time."*

Even existing real estate agents who are floundering in their businesses need to step back and evaluate their current business models. Having a good business plan will help you recognize and determine what changes your business may need.

A properly executed business plan provides many answers for you. For example, who is your target market? What is your value proposition? Do you have a mission statement? And yes, how much money do you need to earn each month to break even? These are just a few of the many questions you will be faced with when creating a business plan.

While we're on the topic of business planning, please keep in mind and understand that this is an ongoing and living piece of work. You should refer to your plan regularly, and make changes and adjustments to your plan as the business environment shifts, your personal life changes, and as other challenges or fluctuations occur within your marketplace.

You should also update your plan annually. Reviewing your business plan yearly is a great way to discover what's working and what's not. By consistently monitoring and updating your business plan, you will be able to answer questions as to where you generate the greatest source of your income and leads. Your business plan will help provide the roadmap and the directions to a successful future as a real estate professional.

> "Your business plan will help provide the roadmap and the directions to a successful future as a real estate professional."

Where and When Do You Begin Your Business Plan?

Constructing a business plan can sometimes be a daunting task. A good time to begin any business planning for the upcoming year is normally in September or October. However, most individuals may first learn they need a business plan in April or even January. Just remember, any time is a good time to start a business plan today! Again, I suggest you consider constructing and reviewing your business plan in September or October. But, by all means, if you just purchased this book and do not have a business plan, start building your plan today! When next September or October arrives, begin to fine-tune your business plan and make any adjustments or changes for the upcoming year, especially since you will now have some experience and understanding of the business and your local market activity.

Where do you begin with building a business plan? A good place to start your plan is by developing a budget. After all, you need to figure out how much money you want to earn to pay your monthly expenses. In the business world, it's called a breakeven analysis. Every real estate professional needs to understand and know how much money he or she needs to earn each month (even annually) in order to pay bills and taxes, and make a profit. Remember from the earlier information in this book, a large percentage of real estate professionals do not even make enough money to pay their normal personal and business expenses.

Wal-Mart and Your Real Estate Business

Many years ago I had the privilege of listening to the founder and CEO of Wal-Mart, Sam Walton, at my university during a business luncheon. It was fascinating to hear Mr. Walton share his visits and trips to the local stores in and around the Cape Girardeau, Missouri area. What I found interesting about Mr. Walton's talk was his description of the department managers who worked for him at the local stores. Mr. Walton was a down-to-earth, good old country boy, who had become successful in promoting discount retailing to small communities.

During his talk at this luncheon, Mr. Walton would refer to his employees and managers as owners of little stores. For example, *Tom has a little fishing store over in Jackson, Missouri. Sherry has a sewing store down in Sikeston, Missouri, and wow, is she doing a great job with her little store!* Mr. Walton would continue, *Dan has a shoe store right here in Cape Girardeau. In fact, Dan was telling me when I visited the store how he needed a certain type of shoe at his store that many of the locals were requesting.* Mr. Walton never referred to these individuals at his Wal-Mart stores as employees but rather as individuals running small businesses (stores right inside the Wal-Mart retail operations). It was interesting and engaging to hear Mr. Walton refer to his employees and managers as storeowners.

Why do I tell the story about Sam Walton's speech and Wal-Mart? First, there's a connection between working for a large organization and running your own real estate business. If you learn to run your business like a business, you will embrace your real estate business more seriously. That was the connection Mr. Walton wanted the audience of small business owners to learn from his presentation. By allowing his employees to take ownership in their departments (their stores), they would work harder for Wal-Mart. If you're just an employee for another organization or company, then how seriously will you work your real estate business?

As real estate professionals, most of you reading this book are operating under independent contractor relationships with your real estate broker. In other words, you are not an employee for the real estate brokerage. Sure, you have obligations, and you must abide by the company's policy and procedures manual, but at the end of the day, it's your real estate business! Since it's your business, developing a business plan is an important first step in your career.

Now that we agree that you own your real estate business, even though you're licensed and positioned under the real estate brokerage license, it's your business reputation. It's your store, as Mr. Walton would remind you. Again, I am not suggesting you can do whatever you want outside the company's normal day-to-day business practices and policy and procedures. You must adhere and follow the rules and regulations of the state real estate commission in your state. Many of you will have obligations through the National Association of REALTORS® code of ethics (if you are a member of the National Association of REALTORS®) and, of course, the company's policies and guidelines. However, you need to remind yourself that you are running your little real estate shop under the brokerage's umbrella! You are responsible for going out and producing listings (properties to sell), finding buyers, and generating income for the company and yourself.

> **It's your little real estate office, so begin running your office today like you own it!**

B.A.S.

How much money do you need to earn to make your real estate business operate successfully? This information is important if you want to get your real estate office off to a good start. I want to share with you a quick and easy way to develop a business plan using an acronym called

B.A.S. (Bachelor of Applied Science). And what is really cool about B.A.S. is that you don't need to have a degree to figure this out. You just need to put a little bit of research and study into preparing and developing a budget.

- B = Budget

- A = Averages for your marketplace

- S = Strategy

To effectively use the acronym B.A.S., you need to gather a few pieces of information. Let's start with B, or budget. There are several sets of numbers you need to obtain to create an effective budget. First, you need to know the amounts that represent all of your monthly obligations or expenses. What is your housing expense? What are your utilities each month? What about your automobile expenses, credit card debt, insurance obligations, dining out and clothing expenses, pharmaceutical requirements, miscellaneous expenses, etc.? It's important to estimate the numbers that represent the amount of monies needed each month to pay all of your monthly obligations. Remember, when you are planning a budget it is always better to be liberal or calculate the expenses at a higher rate than you anticipate spending for the category. For example, it would be better to round your utility expense up to the nearest hundred versus rounding the number downward. After all, this is a budget, and budgets do change over time. But you need to try to estimate as accurately as possible what your monthly expenses might be. You can always come back and make changes later, but for now try to estimate or calculate what your expenses are for a typical month. And yes, you need to calculate and include your real estate business expenses. After all, many of you will have multiple listing service (MLS) dues, your annual REALTOR® dues, or other membership organization fees. You may also have advertising and marketing fees, desk rental costs, lockbox subscriptions, new listing fees and much more. Take your time to develop this list, as this phase toward business planning should be as accurate as possible. Otherwise, your entire projections and planning will be off target.

Sample Expense Budget

Rather than reinventing the wheel, I suggest going to About.com, which offers a sample real estate budget template you can use to begin listing some of the expenses you could incur monthly. I have used this template, and it's wonderful! Here is the link to the budget, but keep in mind, web links do change from time to time, so if you cannot locate it, do a simple search on About.com, or go to Google, Yahoo!®, Bing® or your favorite search engine for a "real estate budget template." Web address for a template: http://realestate.about.com/od/businessstructureandplan/ht/budget_planning.htm

Remember, we're just concentrating and focusing on outflows or expenses each month. If you want to take a moment and begin writing down some of the normal expenses you have that are not included on the worksheet, feel free to do so.

This is also a good time for you to begin thinking about how you will track your expenses for the upcoming year. Hopefully, you are using a good accounting program such as Quicken® or QuickBooks® to record your income and expenses. If not, I encourage you to begin doing so immediately. I also think it's very good for you to make certain when you record deposits and expenses in your accounting software program that you do so as accurately as possible. If you go to the store and you purchase groceries, then categorize that expense as groceries. If the purchase was mainly household cleaning products, list that in the appropriate category. If you can track your expenses for insurance, utilities, groceries, education, automobile and other categories throughout the year, it will be easy to plan and budget for next year and into the future. Having this type of information will allow you to know how much you spend in each one of these categories each month and the entire year. After two or three years, you will be able to predict what you need each month in order to pay your obligations.

Remember, things may change; the economy could go up or down. Catastrophes or other unforeseen situations may arise in your life, but generally you should know where your expenses go each month if you keep good records. In the end, it will help you paint a picture and allow you to determine what your categories will include and what amounts you spend in these areas.

If you're serious about jumpstarting your real estate career in the next five minutes, preparing a budget is the first step of your business plan!

A = Averages

As noted earlier, many of you will be operating as independent contractors. Most independent contractors earn their pay on commission only. There is no weekly or monthly paycheck for the work you perform. If you sell something, you earn a fee (commission). Earning income on a commission-only system is sometimes a difficult concept for many people to get accustomed to, especially if you are used to earning a weekly, biweekly or monthly paycheck from your place of employment.

Having received my license at eighteen, I've lived most of my adult life off of a commission-only status. That's right, no regular paycheck! Some of my months have been home runs while others included grand slams! Still, some weeks, even months, were a series of strikeouts, wondering if I would ever get a hit again. That's part of the real estate sales cycle; you are either on top of the mountain or in the valley. You either hit the ball over the fence, and the crowd erupts into joy, or you go down striking out, walking back to the dugout with your head held low in discouragement.

For most real estate professionals, having a level or a consistent stream of income is a challenge. After all, how can you possibly predict how much money you might earn for the coming year if you do not earn a steady paycheck? One solution is by knowing a little bit about what is going on in your marketplace. If you take the time to study and evaluate what is going on in your marketplace, you can glean some valuable information that will help you prepare for how much money you can earn for the coming year. This exercise will also help you stay focused and possibly avoid many of the slowdowns other real estate agents experience.

In my personal real estate career, I have a short little spreadsheet that tracks all of my buyers, sellers, and closed transactions. I also keep records on how much money I earn from each closed transaction. This data provides me with the average income I earn for each closed transaction. Unfortunately, as a new real estate agent you may not have this luxury of using a previous history of transactions. Keeping good records of your real estate business and your business activities are so important as a real estate professional. Just like keeping track of your expenses is important, understanding and knowing where your business comes from is just as valuable.

My records and information provide me with good data I can use for budgeting and business planning. For example, knowing the average money I earn on the typical transaction is good data to have. If I look back over last year's closed transactions, I can get a gross amount earned. By dividing this number by the total number of transactions for the year, I now have an average per transaction figure that I can use for budgeting purposes. In other words, I can determine how much my average commission check should be for each real estate transaction I close. See the illustration below:

$120,000 Gross Commision Earned → 120 Transactions Closed → $1,000 Earned per Transaction

If I keep these records for two or three years, I can begin to see a trend, and whether my average transaction amount earned is going up or down. This information will help me estimate my earnings when creating a budget and business planning. If I need $10,000 to pay my bills each month, and I'm earning on average $1,000 per closed transaction (from my record keeping) then I know that I need to close ten transactions per month in order to pay my monthly expenses, my taxes and pay myself a profit. You might think, wow, that's 120 transactions per year! Yes, but at least we now know and have some information that will help us develop a plan for achieving the 120 transactions needed to close next year.

How to Calculate Your Average When You Don't Have Data to Use

Some of you may be brand new agents reading this information. In fact, you're probably thinking, "I thought this was a book about five minutes to jumpstarting your real estate career for new agents." Don't worry. I have good news for those of you who are new to the business. When you don't have any data or your own records, you do have data from the local Multiple Listing Service (MLS). Many of you even have your company data to borrow from. If your company has been in business for one or two years, then your broker should have some average commission earned per transaction from the previous year or two. These numbers should help you base your earnings for this exercise.

Before this gets too complicated, I am not asking you to request from your broker what the split or commission exchange is for each agent in your office. Remember, commission splits and payments to agents vary according to the company's policy and procedures, tenure, and many other variables. However, the broker should be able to provide you with what the average sales commission that is earned per transaction, including the broker amount. In other words, the total commission earned per transaction (average commission earned) from the previous year. Having this number will allow you to calculate your portion of the commission from that amount of money earned by the office. For example, if the office's average commission earned for the previous year was $10,000 (per side, i.e., listing side equals $10,000 and buying side equals $10,000) and you are working on a 50/50 split, then your portion per transaction (side) is $5,000. If you had a buyer who purchased from you, you would earn $5,000 (one side). If you had a buyer who purchased one of your listings, you would earn $10,000 (two sides).

Here's another way to calculate the average amount of funds you might earn per transaction closed. First, find out what real estate activity has transpired over the past year in your marketplace.

Let's use this example. If you are a member of the local Multiple Listing Service (MLS) in your marketplace, take the total sales volume last year and divide that by the total number of transactions in your board. I don't want this to be too complicated of a statistical lesson, so I have provided an example from my local MLS below.

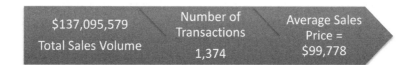

You can now use this average sales price from the board MLS, and apply the commission rate your firm charges to find out the average gross commission earned per transaction per office. Next, multiply your commission split percentage to find out what your average commission check should be based on the previous year's data from your local MLS.

By performing these steps, you will discover what your average fee should be in your marketplace for each side or transaction closed. For example, a salesperson who earns a fifty percent share of his or her broker's commission when the broker charges a six percent marketing fee, based on the $99,778 in my board, would earn $1,496.67 average commission per side/transaction.

12   Chapter 1

$99,778 × .06 = $5,986.68

$5,986.68 / 2 = $2,993.34 (selling office receives 50% and listing office receives 50%)

$2,993.34 / 2 = $1,496.67 (50% to office/broker and 50% to the agent (listing or selling)

Again, the above calculations are based on a six percent sales commission, and the average sales price in my local MLS, with everyone receiving a fifty percent split. As a reminder, commissions are negotiable! Negotiable between offices and the buying and selling public, and negotiable between brokers in the marketplace, as well as brokers and their company agents. The above was only used as an example to help illustrate this point regarding the importance of knowing the "Averages," the "A" in the acronym B.A.S.

As you can see, even a new agent with no track record can glean an approximate amount of money he or she should earn per closed transaction based on the data from the MLS and the local market area. You can also use the total number of closed transactions and divide that by the total number of agents to determine how many transactions, or what the average number of transactions is that are closed per agent in the board. Again I have provided information from my board and the previous year for you below:

What can you learn from all of this? First, these calculations provide you with the average numbers per agent on what is happening in your local marketplace. You should now know what the average sales price is for your market, as well as the average number of transactions per agent. Again, these are "averages," and may or may not be accurate to each agent. However, it does provide you with a good starting point for your business plan. Don't be discouraged if the average number of closed transactions per agent is a bit low, as in the example above for my board. Remember, a lot of agents are underperforming due to several different factors such as working part-time, not maximizing their marketing potential, or a lack of motivation and determination. You do not want to follow the path of the majority in this business. Rather, commit yourself to doing the right activities for becoming a successful real estate professional.

This exercise is also good statistical information for you when you are working with potential clients. When your numbers are much greater or better than the average agent in your board, then use this data to show consumers how many more transactions you close versus the average agent. The bottom line for this exercise is that it provides a good basis for you in preparing your monthly budget.

> "When your numbers are much greater or better than the average agent in your board, then use this data to show consumers how many more transactions you close versus the average agent."

S = Strategy

Now that you have compiled the data and the necessary information to create your budget, it is time to develop your strategy or game plan. Just as your GPS or mapping software will provide an overview of the trip (step by step instructions), you too will need the same type of plan in place for your real estate profession. Let's take a moment and look at a possible plan you might consider implementing to achieve your goals as a new real estate professional.

30 – 10 – 1 Rule

For many years, I have relied on the 30-10-1 rule for reaching my goals. This concept breaks down the following numbers with this plan.

- 30, represents the number of new leads you need to make per closed transaction

- 10, is the number of prospects from the 30 new leads visited who will have an interest in using your services. You might refer to these prospects as "warm" leads

- 1 of the 10 warm leads will buy or sell real estate through you

It's fairly straightforward, and yet a powerful concept to remember. Thirty new leads equals ten warm customers, and one closed transaction!

Let's break down this new plan further. First, presume you have a monthly expense budget of $10,000. In other words, to pay all of your monthly expenses (home and business), pay your required taxes, and put enough money back for a profit, you need to earn $10,000. We arrived at this number by developing a monthly budget, which included everything from your business expenses, including multiple listing fees, association dues, pens, paper, signs, and more. This budget also includes home expenses for insurance, groceries, automobile payment, housing allowance, dining, clothing, etc. After excellent preparation and hard work in constructing your monthly budget, you can safely agree that you need to make $10,000 each month from your real estate activities to pay your expenses, including your taxes, and to earn a profit.

The second step of your budget building and data gathering involves determining what the likely outcome would be for a commission check that is earned within your office. It is important for you to determine past and historical data from either your company, your local MLS, or your own records. This will help you determine what the average amount per commission transaction is that you should earn for your local marketplace. For simplicity's sake we arrive at $1,000 for the average amount of commission earned per closed transaction from the information and research you gathered.

Based on the above information, you can now determine from $10,000 as a required budget amount that is needed, and $1,000 earned per transaction, you will need to close ten transactions per month in order to meet your needs. I realize this might seem like an astronomical number for some individuals, but remember. You need to have a realistic view of what your target goal looks like.

Back to the 30-10-1 rule, and how this can apply to our acronym B.A.S. Knowing you need to make thirty new contacts to receive ten warm leads, and one sale throughout the year will help you develop the plan for your real estate business.

In the previous section, you discovered that you needed to close ten transactions per month to pay your monthly expenses of $10,000. By applying the 30-10-1 rule, you can take 30 × 10 to equal the 300 leads you need to make to meet your monthly quota. Now let's figure that you will work Monday through Friday of a typical week. Nevermind that most real estate agents will normally work more than five days per week. For our example we will calculate a five-day workweek. Using a 30-day month, and four to five weeks each month, we could successfully conclude that you will work approximately twenty-two days out of every month. Remember, you would rather be conservative with your calculations when estimating income, so if you did work more days per month it would only be to your advantage.

Now, let's take twenty-two days divided by 300. To recap, recall that we arrived at 300 by taking the 30 from our 30-10-1 formula and multiplying that by the number of transactions we needed to close. So if you make 30 new contacts according to this formula, you should close one transaction. Thirty leads equate to ten warm leads, and then in turn to one successful sale.

Now, take the 300 needed contacts each month and divide this number by the number of days you plan to work, twenty-two, and you should come up with 13.6. Just to be safe, it would probably be best to round this up to fifteen. You can now conclude that in order to close ten transactions per month, you need to make fifteen new contacts every day throughout the twenty-two days you plan to work each month.

Wow, that may seem like an astronomical number to some folks. Others, may look at the glass as half-full, and be excited to realize that it only requires fifteen new contacts each day to achieve this goal. When you think about this, fifteen contacts can be achieved in as little as thirty minutes, if you went out and visited a neighborhood and began knocking on doors (subdivisions in your community). Yes, you could probably reach your quota, fifteen new contacts, within as little as thirty minutes!

Some of you might be asking the question, what if I live in a small community and I contact all my folks rather quickly? Then simply go back and continue to rework those same leads you've called upon. Remember, even if you are in a small community, you are building your name and reputation as the go-to person for real estate. Trust me. It won't be long until you are considered the real estate expert, and the person who wins most of the real estate business in your market area.

If you are in a larger city or community, you have to focus on getting out and meeting new people every day every day to get the number of people that are required, based on the calculations we just went through using the 30-10-1 rule.

Don't panic. I plan to show you many different ways that you can use your new B.A.S. (Bachelor of Applied Science Degree) and various strategies to grow your real estate business throughout the rest of this book. Most all of the items that I plan to share with you are marketing activities you can do in five minutes or less.

Your plan is important to your success as a real estate professional. And if you follow the suggestions in this chapter of the book, as well as accurately research your marketplace, expenses, etc., you will have the ability to set a target you can reach.

As you can tell, there are a lot of various pieces and parts to an effective and successful business plan. I cannot stress enough how important it is for you as a real estate professional to remind yourself and remember it's your business! If you want to jumpstart your real estate career, you have to begin building a business plan! This plan may not be fun to work on, and it may require hours of research and work, but in the end, it will pay you enormous and sizable dividends.

In 2007, my wife and I went through a challenging life-changing event. In short, I sold my real estate business and took a career in another industry. Within months, I was unemployed and had signed a no-compete clause (remember, real estate is the only career I had ever known since high school), and our pick-your-own blueberry and blackberry crop suffered a late spring freeze. I think you get the picture: no crop, no job, and yes, it was 2007, the beginning of one of the worst real estate cycles in many years.

Rather than sit on the sidelines, my wife and I regrouped, developed our new budget, (in writing) and then set out to create a plan to begin paying back nearly one million dollars in debt that we owed. I am happy to report that we did not have to file bankruptcy, we did survive, and we learned a lot about planning, budgeting, creativity, marketing, persistence and more during this timeframe.

The take-away from my story is two-fold. First, challenges, unexpected happenings, and life in general will not always go as planned. Second, preparing a budget and developing a plan can help create the pathway and vision for where you want to go, and how you plan to get there. Don't let big numbers, daunting circumstances or negative feedback drive your plan. You develop and create your own plan and roadmap to success!

Once you have your marketing and business plan in place, you will normally be updating and changing small portions throughout the year. As noted earlier, changes due to outside forces (higher interest rates, family emergencies, natural disasters in your area, etc.) require revisions. It is important that you block out a few hours regularly, (in a coffee shop or somewhere away from the office) where you can spend time on preparation, planning, and research.

I trust that by following the information laid out in this chapter, you will be able to develop a great business plan to implement with your real estate career. This plan is your road map and guide to success. Feel free to go through the material as a quick and general overview during your first reading, but I strongly encourage you to go back and reread the material, taking the necessary time to construct and build your business plan.

Don't forget, this plan is a living and breathing plan. You will need to evaluate your plan from time to time, and make corrections and changes, and hopefully increase your goals and set your objectives a little higher. I love the quote I heard from a friend of mine who said that, *"If your goals do not make people laugh, then you need to set them higher."* (author unknown)

Though the groundwork and research is now complete, it's now time to get on to what I like to refer to as the fun and exciting strategies for jumpstarting your real estate career in five minutes or less.

Chapter 2

What is **Your Brand?**

Creating a Personal Brand

As I discussed in the previous chapter, your real estate license provides you with the ability to own and operate your own small real estate business. Granted, you are licensed under a designated or principal broker for the firm, but the activities and the building of your career are up to you. As a real estate professional, you should be conscious of reminding yourself that you own and operate your own business. I do not want you to misunderstand the application of the principles in this book, as you must strictly abide by and conform to your company's policy and procedures, and any other requirements they have in place for licensed sales associates within your firm. However, at the end of the day, you need to look at the customers and clients you work with as consumers doing business with your little real estate shop.

Because you need to implement the mindset of being your own small business owner (managing and accounting for all income and expenses incurred daily), it is important for you to apply various marketing strategies and activities that can help grow your business.

Developing a Personal Logo

Have you ever considered developing a personal logo? This is something many successful real estate agents are doing across the U.S. First things first. I must stress the importance of getting any of the ideas and suggestions discussed in this book approved by your associate, managing, or executive broker before utilizing them in your business. Always get the approval of management before implementing any suggested marketing tactics you plan to use. With that being said, creating a brand or logo is one idea you may want to consider. Let's think about some of the benefits of creating a personal logo. First, it can help people remember who you are and what you do. If you read any number of textbooks on marketing and branding, you will find countless examples of authors referring to logos such as Nike®, Disneyland® Park, Coca-Cola®, and others. Companies create logos and develop brands to encourage and help consumers remember their product. By creating a top of mind awareness with a brand or logo, you increase the buyer's awareness of your product or service when they are ready to make a purchasing decision.

If I showed you a red, white, and blue balloon (the RE/MAX® logo), you would immediately recognize and register the balloon with the RE/MAX® brand. For years Century 21® prided themselves and their agents on wearing gold sport coats. In fact, even to this day I can show a friend of mine wearing his gold Century 21 sport coat in an overhead PowerPoint slide presentation, and the audience will immediately call out Century 21, guessing what logo is associated with the company.

Keep in mind that logos are not just for big major corporations. Many real estate professionals (top producing agents) create and use logos throughout their marketing materials. I would encourage you to think about some type of logo that you could incorporate with your real estate career. Specifically a logo that would blend comfortably with a passion or some type of activity that defines you. For example, I use a cartoon character of me teaching in a classroom with the word "technology" in the background. I use this brand because I also teach technology courses to real estate companies and professionals around the world, and it's a passion and interest of mine to help others understand and use technology as real estate professionals.

Figure 2-1   Sample Company Logos – Courtesy of Hobbs/Herder Advertising 800-999-6090.

I have seen other real estate professionals use similar types of logos revolving around fishing, coaching, and much more. Again, the main purpose for creating a logo is to help people quickly and easily put your name with the logo along with the fact that you are in real estate, and they should consider you for their real estate needs. It will also help show a personal side of you as a real estate agent, and associate you with your passion, making it easy to remember you.

It may seem far-fetched, and it will definitely take longer than five minutes for this to register with most consumers in your marketplace. However, implementing and using a professional logo will help you win a tremendous amount of business over time.

Finding a Firm to Develop Your Logo

There are several companies who may develop a personal logo for you, such as Hobbs/Herder, or 99designs.com . You may also hire someone who might be willing to produce a logo from a service like www.elance.com. I have produced several logos for use with my small business activities from a software program called Laughingbird Software (http://www.laughingbirdsoftware.com).

The production of logos can be as simple or as complicated as you like. As referenced earlier in the text, Nike® is one of the most recognizable logos that has established decades of recognition with just a simple swoosh; It actually wasn't even a big marketing or design company that developed the swoosh; it was a college student. So, with just a little creativity and insight into the product you are selling and the message you want to convey, you can come up with a memorable logo. The most important thing to remember, especially during the time you are starting up your own business, is that expensive does not always equate to effective. A design can also be created by utilizing a basic program such as Microsoft Paint® that is included free on many computers. For those agents who have any experience with Adobe® products, such as Adobe® and Photoshop®, you can use this program to create some interesting and effective logos.

After you have developed your personal logo, remember to incorporate your logo with all of your marketing activities. Your logo should be incorporated within your email signature, your marketing flyers, envelopes, stationery, and of course your website. I have watched many good sales associates develop a wonderful logo and a specific branding statement only to halfheartedly incorporate it with their marketing. This is your brand, and you should use your logo with all of your marketing materials.

I recall working with a franchise organization for a short period of time during my no-compete period, and witnessing the majority of the agents omitting the use of the franchise logo. Whether your logo is a personal logo you create, or a company logo, use it! It is important to create a synergy and strategy of incorporating and using your logo on each and every piece of marketing material you produce.

> **"Whether your logo is a personal logo you create, or a company logo, use it!"**

Many real estate brokers may not appreciate or agree with my following statements about why I believe an individual logo is important for you as a sales associate. Remember, your logo does not need to be tied directly with the company logo. Let me try to explain this further. First, you definitely want your logo to convey that you are in real estate. You also want to make certain the logo does not overpower your company brand. You should also get approval from management before you have a logo created.

The unfortunate reality is that real estate offices will come and go. You may also find yourself in need of a change of scenery. Yes, real estate agents do change real estate brokerages. According to the National Association of REALTORS®, and their 2014 Profile of Real Estate Agents, the average stay at a real estate office has declined to six years. Also, from that same profile, nine percent of real estate agents indicated their company was either purchased or merged with another firm during the last two years.

Some real estate agents may even decide they want to open a real estate brokerage (sorry brokers and managers, but if you have been in this business for any length of time, you know this is a hard, cold fact that we must acknowledge and accept). Because of these reasons and others, if your logo is too constricted or confined and incorporates the current brand, retooling or changing your logo two or three years down the road will be a difficult task. After all, creating your personal brand and logo may take years to take root in your local marketplace. If your logo completely incorporates or uses the current brand or logo of the firm or franchise, you may find yourself in big trouble when you need to make a change or are forced to make a change.

Remember to sit down with your broker and discuss your desires and the idea of creating a personal logo. Follow the rules and procedures and any policies the company requires for using a personal logo. And if your company does not allow a personal logo, it's not the end of the world. It's just an idea or a suggestion for you to consider. It may also be a question to ask various brokers when you are interviewing to work for a particular agency when starting your new career.

As a real estate broker and owner of a real estate company, I have always wanted my sales agents to stay with me for eternity. Unfortunately, some of my best sales agents wanted to start their own company. Others did not like new changes or policies that I enforced. Some felt better to make a change to a new company to help their careers. In fact, as noted earlier, even I sold my brokerage at one point, and the new owner did not want to use the existing logo or name (used for twenty-six years in the local marketplace) forcing everyone in the company to retool. Yes, even my agents were forced to change their e-mail addresses and other information to a totally different brand to the marketplace. The bottom line is to keep your logo personal and easily transferable. You never know when you may find yourself in a new territory or with a new company.

Mission Statement – And Your Brand

You may also consider creating a mission statement as we discussed in the business planning chapter. If so, how can your mission statement be tied into your logo or brand?

What is your value proposition? Again, from the business chapter, refer back to and think about some of the value propositions you plan to bring to the marketplace. How can you tie in those specific value added services that you will provide buyers and sellers with your logo and slogan? Speaking of slogans, have you developed any type of a personal slogan for your business? Oftentimes you can have a logo created with a short slogan or tagline underneath, so that consumers will associate the slogan or tagline with you, your logo, and real estate. This is another way people can remember you and what business you are in.

Finally, make sure your logo is professional! Some of the logo companies I mentioned will provide you with two or three samples to choose from. Share these proofs with your broker and others in the office to get their input. It's always a good idea to make certain your logo and brand reflect a professional image that your firm and you plan to display in your local community. Also, if you are an existing agent reading this book and looking for ways to jumpstart your real estate career, you might consider having your personal logo updated or enhanced if you currently have one.

I used a logo for many years that my mother created when she first started her real estate firm. After approximately twenty-two years, I realized the logo needed to be updated and re-tooled. It cost me several thousand dollars to have a new logo developed, including replacing signs, stationary and other marketing pieces for the company. Still, this was probably one of the best decisions I have made.

Think about some of the larger corporations in the marketplace and how they go through re-branding and retooling every ten to twenty years. Taco Bell, Wal-Mart, Wendy's, KFC—all of these companies and many others understand that their logo and brand may need to change or be updated over time.

The following pages provide various examples of real estate agents and personal branding throughout the United States. I appreciate each agent and company listed for allowing me to include his or her artwork, brand, logo, and slogans in my book. I have provided a link to their websites and contact information, should you need more questions answered. Remember, some of the web links or companies may change over time, so if you are not able to locate someone mentioned in this book, please accept my apologies.

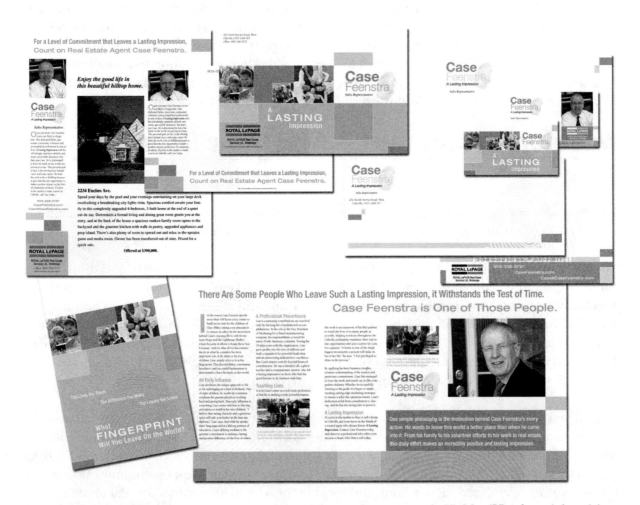

Figure 2-2 Case Feenstra Marketing Materials – Courtesy of Hobbs/Herder Advertising 800-999-6090.

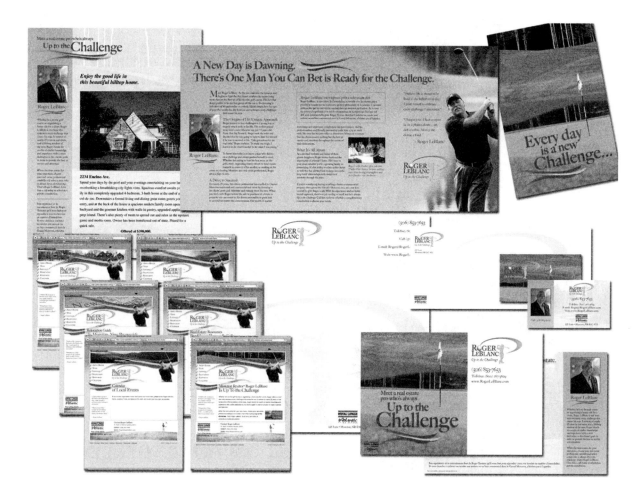

Figure 2-3 Roger LeBlanc Marketing Materials - Courtesy of Hobbs/Herder Advertising 800-999-6090.

Figure 2-4 Islay Lamb Marketing Materials – Courtesy of Hobbs/Herder Advertising 800-999-6090.

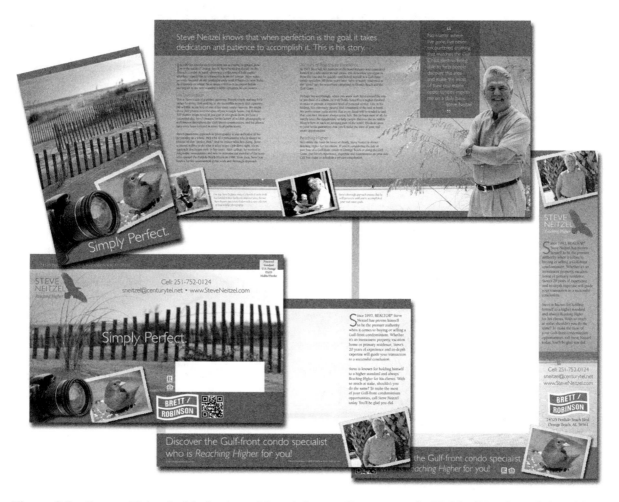

Figure 2-5 Steve Neitzel Marketing Materials – Courtesy of Hobbs/Herder Advertising 800-999-6090.

Chapter 3

Create a Niche to
Help Build Your Brand

Niche Marketing

One area real estate agents often fail to utilize is the concept of Niche Marketing. According to **http://www.merriam-webster.com/dictionary/niche**, niche is defined as:

a place, employment, status, or activity for which a person or thing is best fitted, a specialized market.

Sometimes creating a niche or specialty in a specific segment of your marketplace can be a good way to win business. If you sold homes in a lake and resort area, and you were the *"lakefront home specialist,"* you could easily brand and position yourself to win a larger percentage of the lakefront homes in your development.

Consider the agent who specializes in the Whispering Pines Subdivision: by including this statement or specialty within your marketing materials and promoting yourself as the expert in Whispering Pines, you may soon be the go-to person for real estate in this subdivision.

Understand that just because you include yourself as an expert with your marketing and branding, does not preclude you from doing business in other areas of your marketplace. After all, just because you may specialize in Whispering Pines Subdivision does not necessarily mean this is the only place you do real estate transactions. A first-time homebuyer's specialist may also work with repeat buyers. VA or Government specialty real estate professionals may be involved in just as many conventional loan transactions. Still, there is something unique and mysterious to the general public when they see an ad or marketing piece showcasing a person who focuses on a specific niche. Many consumers want to do business with someone who is an expert in a specific field or area where they plan to do business.

It only makes sense that if you were going to have heart surgery that you would want a heart specialist to operate on your heart. This leads to a very important point regarding the creation of a niche, especially if you plan to advertise your specialty to the buying and selling public. If you do plan to take it upon yourself to create a niche, you should make it a point to become as familiar and knowledgeable as you can about your specialty topic. I would never encourage anyone to make a marketing claim about being the expert for Whispering Pines Subdivision, unless he or she indeed made it a point to study and know the Whisperings Pines Subdivision, frontwards and backwards.

If you are a lakefront home specialist, you should take the necessary steps to learn the proper information about owning a home on the water because, again, adding the word "specialist" to your business card does not necessarily make you one. For example, if you seek to be a waterfront or lakefront specialist, it would be advisable for you to learn all aspects of this type of ownership that often affect your area, such as flood zones, the specifics of property lines in and around water, water easements, etc. These issues are often big factors when clients are buying properties that are located by, or including, water. Knowing about these varying factors would never eliminate your responsibility as an agent to tell your client to consult an expert in the proper field of study if one of these factors may exist, but it would enable you to let your client know that some of these factors may exist in the purchase of a specific property when otherwise they may not know.

My point is this; always be open and honest when creating a niche or claiming expert status when you broadcast your message to the general public.

Pick a Niche You Enjoy

The second idea you should remember regarding the creation of a niche is that it only makes sense to focus on a specialty in which you have an interest. If you want to be a VA home loan specialist for military homebuyers, then you need to enjoy doing these types of transactions. If you advertise yourself as a farm and land expert, you should like selling farms and land. It only makes good common sense to develop a niche or specialty within an area in which you have an interest and/or a passion to work.

With that being said, niche marketing can be a profitable venture. By spending the proper time, research and education, you will begin to know a specialized area better than anyone else in your marketplace. You will also begin to develop ideas and suggestions on how you can market yourself in specific niche areas.

> **"Only pick a niche in which you have an active interest in pursuing and enjoy."**

Pick a Niche That Is Profitable

You should also pick a niche within your marketplace that is profitable. Naturally, you would not want to pick a specialty that has very little activity in your marketplace. Even though there is nothing wrong with pursuing a niche in a market area that you have a passion or interest, if there is virtually no business to be made within this niche market, then it would probably do you no good to pursue this type of marketing activity. For example, I have a passion and desire to sell properties along the Gulf of Mexico. However, being in Missouri (in the middle of the United States), this type of niche real estate segment does me no good. Okay, I probably took the example a little too far, but I think you understand what I'm trying to convey. Only develop a niche in your marketplace where there is a demand or need for that type of specialty real estate service.

If you begin to think about the various types of niche marketing available, the list can become quite extensive.

Niche Real Estate Marketing Ideas

- First-time home buyers
- Buyers only
- Sellers only
- Military Specialist
- Farms and Land
- Waterfront
- Condos
- Vintage
- Victorian
- Subdivision Specialist
- 1031 Exchange
- Investment
- Foreclosure, bank owned
- Short-sale specialist
- Green (Environmental) expert
- Senior adults
- Relocation
- People in transition (loss of spouse or divorce situation)
- Downtown or city expert
- Lofts

Niche marketing may not be for everyone, but it does provide an excellent marketing advantage over real estate professionals who make no attempt to differentiate themselves from the competition. If you do plan to create a niche or become a specialist in a specific area, I would encourage you to tie this in with your brand and logo, and especially your slogan! You definitely want to make certain that your logo, brand, and slogan all do a good job conveying to the consumer your specific area of expertise.

> **"If possible, combine your niche with your logo, brand, or slogan."**

Finally, don't worry about trying to create a niche tomorrow or the next day. In fact, you may not fully understand or know yet what area of specialty you want to concentrate on until you have been practicing in the marketplace for some time. Nevertheless, I do want you to be aware of the opportunities niche marketing can create, and have you think about the possibilities where you may want to focus your real estate career as it develops and grows.

Chapter 4

Systems and Checklists to
Operate Your Business Efficiently

Systems and Checklists

It is a great accomplishment to jumpstart your real estate career in a short period of time. Still, in order to witness an optimum level of success and take your real estate profession to the next level, I believe you must have good systems in place. Sadly, many real estate professionals attempt to run their real estate careers in a haphazard fashion. Don't get me wrong. I'm not trying to talk disparagingly about my fellow real estate colleagues, but, unfortunately, most agents do not have good systems and checklists in place. Successful top-producing real estate individuals and teams that I know operate their businesses with systems and checklists.

What do I mean by checklists and systems? First, you need to have a series of tasks and functions for each particular phase of the real estate transaction. It also goes much deeper than this, whereas each transaction has various phases and steps. The same is true of your checklists and action plans. Each corresponding phase to the transaction should have a series of tasks or a checklist that you can use to make certain nothing falls between the cracks. For example, what are the processes each time you acquire a new listing for a seller? What about the various tasks needed when a buyer finalizes an accepted contract? Each type of real estate transaction has a multitude of action items that are required for a successful completion.

Several years ago I was having dinner with one of the top ten real estate agents for a well-known international real estate franchise. We will call my friend Rick. I asked Rick during dinner if there was one particular item that was beneficial to his real estate success. Without blinking an eye, or any hesitation in his voice, Rick immediately shared his success secret. *"If it had not been for setting up good systems and checklists, my business would not be where it is today,"* Rick told me.

> *"If it had not been for setting up good systems and checklists, my business would not be where it is today."*
>
> —*Top sales agent for a national franchise.*

One reason a checklist is important is because of the number of items normally associated with a real estate transaction. Let's examine a series of activities you may need to do when you earn a new listing for a seller.

Date	Task	Completed
	Placement of for sale sign	
	Placement of lock box	
	Paperwork complete	
	Entered into MLS	
	Added to website	
	Photos complete	
	YouTube video created	
	Advertising copy completed	

Date	Task	Completed
	Extra keys made for office	
	Scheduled open house	
	Send thank you card to seller	
	Posted on social media	
	File submitted to office	
	Scheduled first follow-up with client	
	(And many more items to be added)	

As you can see, there are various tasks and items that need to be followed and completed any time you obtain a new listing, and my list is only a small sample of what is normally required when most agents take a new listing. Your company or broker may have more items than what I have listed. You will also have additional tasks and items to perform when your listing sells or it is no longer available for sale. Without checklists to remind you of every item that needs to be completed, various tasks could slip through the cracks. For example, if you add a video to YouTube, that video needs to be removed once the listing is no longer a part of your inventory. Checklists help you stay reminded of what you need to do for all of your real estate business.

Think about how checklists can help you build your personal reputation as a real estate professional. Compile a list of utility services for your buyers after the sale. Follow up with your listing clients regularly throughout the listing period, enhancing the level of communication and service you provide to your clients. Follow up with past clients and customers after the closed transaction to ensure they will remember you and refer you to other friends and family members for real estate needs. Checklists enable you to stay on track and be certain each and every detail is never missed.

Another important reason for checklists is to help establish the habit of maintaining logs on what transpired during your work activities while you support your clients and customers. The issue of liabilities should not stop a prospective agent from pursuing a career in real estate, but it should always be a concern. With preventative measures—such as keeping checklists and noting the date and time of each item accomplished, as well as keeping notes as much as possible regarding conversations with clients—you it will eliminate a lot of "he said/she said" issues that could come up later. For example, if you have a conversation with a client on June 10th regarding the requirement to have a building inspection completed within seven days, if an issue arises where the seven-day period lapses, and the client claims to have been misinformed in any way, you have the documentation to support your conversation. Plus, your checklist would also have a reminder for you, one or two days prior to the seven-day clause, to follow-up on the inspection to ensure all deadlines are met in a timely manner.

Documentation is one of the most important proactive and preventative habits you can learn as a real estate professional. Top professionals in the industry often use the term "Document, document, document."

Social Media Checklist

Recently, I began to think about my social media strategy and some of the videos and blog posts that I was providing on my website. As I was in my car on my way to a new appointment, I began to remember various tasks in social media sharing features that I had forgotten to include with my blog post. Because of these leaks in my social media strategy, I decided to sit down and construct a social media strategy checklist. I prepared a checklist in Microsoft Word® and then saved the document as a PDF (portable document file). I then converted the PDF into a fillable form. Creating a fillable checklist form helps me keep a task list on my computer. You can easily create a checklist in programs similar to Evernote™, which I will discuss in more detail later. Each time I engage with a new social media activity, I can check off the various tasks and then save this form in the appropriate folder on my computer.

When I first began constructing this checklist, my original tasks were eight or nine items that needed to be completed. However, after I continued to ponder and think about the various social media strategies, it was not long until I quickly developed twenty various social media action items—everything from posting to Instagram, adding specific copy and changing the copy to YouTube, posting to Facebook, Twitter, etc. Believe it or not, every time I create a video, blog post, or podcast, there are some twenty different action items associated with this online marketing strategy. I quickly realized how many required tasks there were for one social media activity. By incorporating a social media strategy checklist, I can quickly go through all of the items that need to be done and ensure nothing is left out. After all, if you want to make certain your social media activity reaches a larger footprint on the Internet, you must place your information on as many sources as possible. My social media strategy checklist has become beneficial, assisting me with making certain I don't miss any tasks.

I would encourage you to create your checklists in a program such as Microsoft Word® or Evernote™ and then take your lists, and if possible, create the lists for fillable PDF documents. There are several solutions available for creating fillable PDF's. I would suggest that you save your PDFs and checklists within each folder on your computer. You can find out more information about organizing and filing your information in the next chapter on organization and filing.

Finally, get in the habit of creating checklists and developing systems for each aspect of your real estate business. Checklists are a critical step to success, and one specific activity that will help you jumpstart your real estate career in five minutes!

Chapter 5

Organization and Filing for the
Real Estate Professional

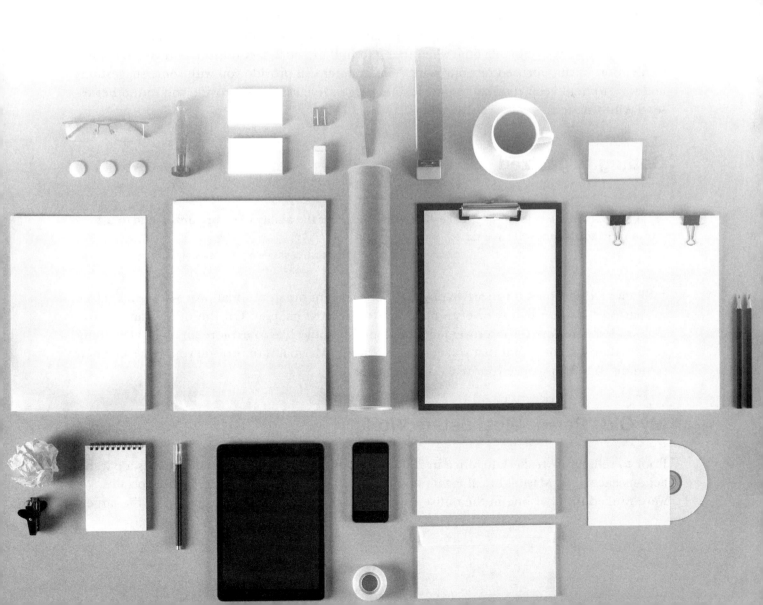

Organization

Imagine walking into a cluttered room years after its last cleaning. Clothes are all over the floor, objects and debris are everywhere—a chaotic mess! Now imagine yourself trying to sit down at a desk in this room, after spending fifteen to twenty minutes removing the stacks of papers to find just enough space you can comfortably use. Finally, try to imagine sitting in this messy room and writing letters to some of your clients and customers. It might be a challenging task to work in such an environment.

Now let's think about your five goals written on a piece of paper. Unfortunately, this paper is somewhere underneath all the rubble and debris. How could you work in this type of setting, and how could you focus on your written goals? In fact, would your written goals allow you to stay motivated and focused on your desired outcome? Probably not. After all, you cannot even locate your goals inside this room full of papers.

I realize I'm taking this cluttered room example to the extreme. However, if your organizational habits are not what they should be for your real estate files and information, you are probably going to lose a lot of valuable time when trying to find the necessary information you need, not to mention staying focused on your work. This chapter will provide you with some suggestions and ways to help keep your real estate business organized, as well as provide you with other essential information.

Getting Organized

> "A big part of success for any real estate organization is the ability to be organized and to use the right tools that will save time."

I will give a disclaimer: if you are happy with your current organizational process, then feel free to read this chapter lightly or even move on to the next chapter. On the other hand, if you believe there is room for improvement and you also would like to explore an alternative filing system, then I recommend that you continue reading. My goal is to provide you with some new solutions to help organize your real estate business.

My Old "Paper" Real Estate World

Prior to selling my real estate office in 2006, the company was closing a lot of real estate transactions each year. Mayfield Real Estate had three offices and close to forty sales associates. We were ranked number one in the entire county for production, and number two in the largest city in the area. It is probably needless to point out that having our paperwork organized and easy to get to was important.

Unfortunately, even with all of the great methods I felt I had implemented for organizing in a paper world, things were a bit spread out and crazy. Many states have specific rules and regulations pertaining to the agency and how sales associates within the office can view files or paperwork. I won't bore you with all of the details about designated agency in Missouri. I will only tell you that if your office chooses to operate as a designated agency, you cannot leave folders and important documents open for anyone who is a licensed agent at your company to view, unless of course he or she is involved in the transaction and appointed the designated agent for the client.

Because of this complex process, our records were spread out in various places throughout our office. Expired listings were in the attic (and it was a dreaded task to have to go and get an old file out of one of the expired boxes on a July afternoon). Pending and under contract files were locked up in my office, and the active listings were situated next to my assistant. Oh, and by the way, not every piece of important information could be kept in the active listing file. Therefore, those documents were required to be locked up in my office as well. Just typing this information reminds me of how crazy and complicated organizing real estate files can be.

As I noted earlier, I sold my real estate office in 2006. It took my wife and me three full days to move all the the paperwork from my real estate office to a storage locker, where they would need to be kept for another three years. We couldn't believe the amount of papers and boxes we moved to this storage locker.

I still had a strong desire to go back in the real estate business, but I promised my wife that if I did reopen an office, I was going to do things differently. I also informed her that I wanted to become a paperless office. She kind of snickered at me because she knew how cluttered and messy my desk and files had become through my normal business practices. I told her to give me a chance because I knew paperless solutions, and mobile paperless offices were the future in real estate.

A period of three years passed while I waited for my "no compete" clause to expire. A no compete clause in real estate is similar to a no compete clause in other businesses. It prevents agents and brokers from taking the clients or trade secrets they attained from the brokerage where they were previously affiliated.

I was also doing some speaking about how to go paperless in my technology seminars and was intrigued with setting up a system I could use. I realized that I needed to practice what I was preaching, so I set up a paperless real estate office and began scanning all of my documents. At first I was trying to go back and scan everything. But I quickly realized that would take too much time, so I decided to move my office into a paperless world from that date forward. I mention this because I believe sometimes people want to go paperless, but they believe they should go back and try to scan all of their previous documents and records. I suggest leaving those documents where they are and beginning to scan when you choose to go paperless. You can and should scan all of your active files, but I would not worry about or attempt to go back and scan previously closed files and paperwork. It simply is too much time and work!

What I discovered over the next few months was simply mind-boggling. First, my desk became clean and the stacks of paper were gone. I was able to find information quickly and easily. Where once I spent much of my time searching for specific papers, I was now working and accomplishing more tasks throughout my day. In all honesty, I was suddenly operating at an efficiency that I had never seen in my real estate career. This is why I believe going paperless is so important. Granted, there are security issues involved, and going paperless may not be for everyone, but it is a method of organization you may want to consider.

Even today, I have files and documents at my fingertips, whether I am at my office, in the field, or half way around the world. I recall one speaking trip that recently took me to France. While there, I needed to send an important file from a closed transaction to a client. It was vital that he receive this specific paper ASAP. I received his call in France, and within minutes delivered a copy of the requested document to him via e-mail. Remember, in my previous real estate career, that sold file would have been buried within a pile of boxes and folders in the attic of my office. But now, with a few keystrokes on my computer and a search for the client's name, the document was retrieved (in France) and sent directly to my client. Going paperless has definitely supported my work/life balance and allowed me to enjoy a more fun and fuller life.

Go Paperless

My first suggestion for you as a real estate professional is to be sure to learn a little bit about filing information on your computer. I will discuss some basic hard copy filing in the next section, but I believe you should take the time to organize your files on your computer, preferably with an online cloud storage portal. Using a cloud-based system will help you with accessing your information from your local computer, as well as from remote locations and mobile devices as noted in the previous section. There are several methods for accomplishing this task; some involve using the Internet (cloud) and some involve using paper. However, I encourage you to consider the ability to store your information on a remote (secure) server if at all possible. I will discuss more of this throughout the chapter.

I also recommend keeping one folder on your desktop or in your documents folder labeled "real estate business or clients." This folder will then contain three additional folders inside of its location.

I like to create folders inside my real estate files folder with my client's last name, first name, and property address.

Keeping your folders within one folder provides several benefits and features. First, you're assured that one main directory or folder, entitled "Real Estate Business," stores all of your data.

Having one general folder makes it easy for you to copy this folder to an external hard drive or a specific backup location. You might also consider having this folder located or linked to a folder inside a program like Evernote™, Dropbox, or Google Drive. This process allows you access to this information from your mobile phone, tablet, or another device that has connectivity to the Internet. I can assure you that this has been beneficial for me. Once, while attending a closing, the escrow agent (closer) was missing a file. She had specific instructions not to disburse the seller's proceeds or finalize the closing without all the proper papers on her checklist. No disbursement also means you will not receive a commission check! The worst part was for the sellers, who wanted their proceeds from the closing right then. Normally, I would have had to leave the building, get in my car, and go back to my office to retrieve the necessary documents we were missing. As a side note, the cooperating broker had his file folder, but he was also missing the specific document the lender was requesting. Because I operate in a paperless office environment, I was able to pull the specific document up from my smart phone and email a copy to the closing officer right from the closing table. Within seconds, she had the paper and was able to finalize the transaction and disperse all of the proceeds, including my commission check! Again, without an organized system linked to the Internet, I would have had no choice but to drive across town to my office, delaying our closing by at least one-half hour.

Having your files organized on your computer and linked to the Internet also makes it easy to find the information you need. Since most computers will allow you to search by keywords, you can easily type in a few letters or words and find a list of all the documents on your computer hard drive that match your search string. If you can get in the habit of organizing your information in the same specific way, it will make finding the data and information a breeze. For example, I always label my information with what the specific file contains first: Sales Contract, Smith, John and Mary, 510 Any Street St., Anytown, MO 63640. From the saved search string, you can see that I renamed (or saved) the file by what the document is, the customer or client's last name, followed by their first name, and the property address.

It's easy to find documents I need. For example, I can simply type "Smith" into my computer search bar, or I can go to my real estate office files folder and quickly glance down alphabetically to the Smith folder.

Having your information organized and easily accessible will save you valuable time and allow you the opportunity to be focused on doing the things you need to be doing: prospecting, presenting, and closing transactions!

Security and Back-Up

If you do plan to go paperless, you definitely need to consult with an Internet or web master security advisor. Making certain that your data is secure from hackers and outside sources is critical. Remember, you are going to be hosting a lot of private and valuable information about clients and customers who do business with you. One breach, and your company could be involved in a public relations nightmare.

> "Remember, you are going to be hosting a lot of private and valuable information about clients and customers who do business with you. One breach, and your company could be involved in a public relations nightmare."

There are some basic steps and procedures to follow to make certain your data is safe and secure. First, you need a good policy and procedures manual for all record keeping. Hopefully, your broker or company has policies in place for paperless solutions, if not, encourage your broker to do so immediately.

Second, have a secure and challenging password. Normally, your password should be twelve characters or more and should include symbols and letters. A combination of upper and lower-case letters works well for security measures. You should also change your passwords regularly!

Third, subscribe to a service such as Carbonite, where your files can be backed up instantaneously to their server. Carbonite® isn't very inexpensive, but it's worth every penny because I know that my files and information are securely backed up to a remote location. Just yesterday, I heard a man sitting next to me on a plane talking to one of his employees just before takeoff. The employee's laptop computer had been stolen, and unfortunately, since his files had not been backed up, all his files and notes were gone as well. The man assured his employee that there was no need to worry about the computer, as it could be replaced. But there was obviously nothing that could be done about the files.

With a subscription to Carbonite®, all of the files from that laptop computer would have been backed up to the cloud. Even if someone had stolen his laptop, he could have recovered all of his files and data through Carbonite®. This person could have also used a program called LoJack® with his laptop computer. This computer system allows LoJack® the ability to add a poison pill to the laptop destroying all of the information the next time the computer logs onto the Internet. It can also assist police departments on locating the stolen computer equipment.

Finally, you should make certain that you are careful when you are on Wi-Fi networks, downloading information, and a slew of other safety precautions I discuss during my live technology seminars I present on this topic. Internet security is a big issue for companies today, and if you plan to go paperless, you should make certain that the windows and doors to your technology are locked, and will prevent thieves from gaining access to your files. Your clients have every legal right to have their personal information protected that is stored in your files.

Paper Files

If you plan to operate in a paper world, invest in a good filing system where you can organize the information accordingly. I would suggest a real estate closing folder system. You can normally find these by doing a search on your favorite Internet search engine, and typing in "Real Estate

Closing Folders." I also like using a good self-adhesive fastener system for my paper files. I then try to organize the paperwork in a specific and consistent procedure. In other words, if your miscellaneous paperwork is at the bottom of your file, then you have the sales contract, followed by any disclosures, the closing statements, etc., You should then follow this same method of organization for each paper file. It will make it much easier to find the documents in the file when you need them.

Whatever method you choose with regards to a paper system or an online filing method, make sure you spend time developing a format that works best for you. Setting this up correctly in the beginning will help you to stay organized as a real estate professional.

Organizing Letters and Other Information on Your Computer

As we discussed in a previous chapter, systems and action plans are very important for the real estate professional. Business correspondence is also an important issue that real estate agents should spend time putting together appropriately and correctly. Having access to various letters and email templates you regularly use can be a huge benefit. Staying organized with your daily communication needs will also save you valuable time each and every day. In my previous two books, *5 Minutes to a Great Real Estate Letter* and *5 Minutes to More Great Real Estate Letters,* my goal was to encourage and help real estate professionals have quick access to professionally written letters and email templates. I am a big proponent of making certain your letters and emails look professional! I will also tell you that I practice what I preach, and I continue to use many of the letters and email templates in my books every day. You can purchase these books and others from my website, www.BusinessTechGuy.com, or from your favorite bookstore.

Here's my suggestion for organizing your letters and other correspondence on your computer. First, make a list of the letters and emails that are appropriate for your business, and that you plan to use regularly. Next, save the letters and email templates within folders on your computer desktop, and label this folder "Real Estate Letters" or "Business Letters and Correspondence."

Having access to this folder on your desktop will allow you to open the folder, find the correspondence, copy the text, and paste it into your new document.

Your only other task is to customize the letter to the specific individual or individuals to which you are sending the letter or email. I have also purchased two software programs that I use. Whether you are a Windows® or Mac® user, you can streamline the writing process even faster than described above. Currently, I use a software vendor called TextExpander®. With TextExpander®, I can create what are called snippets. Snippets have labels, and the labels allow you to type a few keystrokes (tymay1), and TextExpander® will then auto-complete the text you have assigned to the label. For example, if you want to send a thank-you-for-listing letter, you simply type the letters tymay1, and TextExpander® will paste the information in whatever program you are using. In fact, it will paste the assigned text in your email program, or any other text block you have open on your computer. This software program is similar to what we would call running a macro in the older days of computer jargon. A macro provides the computer with instructions on what to type and what keystrokes to perform. If you want to type any letter or phrase, paragraph, etc., you can type it once into TextExpander®, give the assigned text some specific shortcut label, save the snippet, and then perform this task whenever you type the assigned label.

Talk about saving time, TextExpander® is one of my all-time favorite productivity tools! Don't panic if you are a Windows® user, a program called ShortKeys provides the same timesaving functions. Both websites provide detailed information about how the programs work; plus, you can always go to YouTube and type in more information about TextExpander® or, "how does ShortKeys for Windows work?" You should find many video tutorials to help enlighten you and help you understand how the software programs work.

> **"Organization and working in an environment that is easy for you to access files, lookup data and write or create emails and letters with only a few keystrokes is a must."**

Keeping organized will also provide you with the proper direction and setup for succeeding in jumpstarting your real estate career.

Chapter 6

Presentations with Pizzazz

Presentations

Opportunities decline and rise in real estate from time to time, and as an agent and a broker for many years, I have definitely had my share of peaks and valleys. I knew I had to increase my efforts in new directions to balance with the times in order to keep the momentum going. The surge in advanced technology that became more readily accessible around the early 2000s, during the economic downturn our country experienced, was definitely one of those declining times.

My wife and I once had a conversation about a possible listing I had lost. I told my wife how rusty and outdated I felt in my attempts to go out and win real estate business. I think I may have told her I was not cut out for a career in real estate anymore, and I had lost my magic touch for winning listings from for-sale-by-owners and other real estate prospects. My wife quickly reminded me of a fancy little electronic gadget that I carry with me almost every place I go, including my listing appointments. Yes, it is the iPad®, and I use this gadget for many various business functions. I asked my lovely wife what she meant by that reminder. She quickly responded, *"You have that fancy little electronic gadget. Are you using it when you talk to customers about possibly listing their properties?"*

I had a queasy feeling in my stomach as she questioned me about my iPad® and about using it as a device to visually tell my story. Here I am, a technology speaker and a real estate instructor who helps other individuals with their prospecting and training needs. I was preaching something in the pulpit, but I wasn't practicing it in real life! I encouraged and advocated other sales associates to use some type of a presentation aid in their businesses, but I was not using a presentation in my own career. As an experienced agent, I didn't consider the need for a presentation device, or even a paper presentation program when visiting and talking to potential customers. I was simply trying to win business through verbal presentations, which does not work. Trust me; it's hard for people to understand and remember all of your benefits and accolades, or to make note of all they receive from you in an oratory presentation.

After my wife's advice, I quickly sat down and put together a PowerPoint® presentation about my company and myself. There are many different tools and programs that can be utilized to design presentations that offer a professional look with pizazz. PowerPoint® seems to be the most popular among agents because of its ease of use and crisp designs. Prezi® is another program that is often utilized for presentations. Prezi® is an online software program that offers more movement options in your presentation than PowerPoint®. You can find out more about Prezi® at www.prezi.com.

Due to the fact that PowerPoint® is the most widely used software for business presentations, I will address some of the do's and don'ts of that program here. Most of these rules are overall design rules, so they can also be applied to Prezi® or any other presentation design program. Making your presentations more streamlined and professional-looking is the best way to get your client's attention and place your best foot forward.

One of the most important tips to using PowerPoint® or any other presentation program is to avoid having cluttered slides. Having too many lines, bullets, or images on a slide can make a viewer busy reading and trying to decipher the information, instead of listening to what you are saying. For that same reason, make sure that your slides complement what you are saying while the slide is up. It is not necessary for you to say exactly what is on the slide. A presentation is much more interesting and engaging for viewers when they aren't given all of the information both ways. For example: if you are talking about the skillsets you have to offer a client, including availability, education, and years in the business, you might have it appear on a slide as follows:

- Availability

- Education

- Years in the Business

When you are speaking, you would say each of the terms but extend on each of the bullets verbally. When discussing "availability," you would explain what times you are available and how often you check your emails and texts. For "education," you would talk about how much education in the real estate market you have had, and for "years in the business," you would talk about how many years you have spent in the business. With the visual clues and verbal explanations, you are engaging the viewer in both visual and verbal material, increasing your chances of appealing to more types of sensory learners.

In order to avoid a lot of clutter on each slide, it is best to limit your bullets to three or four lines, at the most, per slide, with a limited amount of words per line. This gives the presentation more punch and less opportunity for the viewer to read ahead and miss the information you are covering within the presentation. When utilizing images on your slides, try not to use more than one per slide and use images that are as professional-looking and creatively done as possible. This will complement your overall first impression with future clients.

It was amazing when I began to think about all of the various tools and features that I would be providing to my potential sellers, and how I would be marketing their properties if they chose me as their real estate professional. Once I completed the presentation, I loaded it on my iPad® and rehearsed and practiced it as if I were in front of potential clients.

I called on an expired listing in my hometown, and the customers invited me over for a quick preview. As I arrived at the house and we toured the property, it wasn't long before the sellers began to tell me some of their frustrations and dissatisfaction with their previous real estate company. Without mentioning anything derogatory against my competitor (which I would never encourage or advise anyone to do) I simply asked the sellers if I could show them how my company is different from my competitors. I was ready and prepared to use my iPad® to visually explain some of the ways that I would market their property, and a few other benefits my company had to offer. I have included a copy at the end of this chapter for you to review. My presentation covers most of my essential talking points: my company history, a little bit about me, and then specific details for buyers and sellers. I believe your main goal with your PowerPoint® is to help answer questions the potential client may have. Buyers want and need to know about pre-qualification, having inspections performed, and how long the process may take. Sellers will want to know where you intend to market their property, where buyers come from, and how long their property might be for sale. Both buyers and sellers need to know a little bit about the negotiation phase, contracts, and who represents whom.

As we sat down at their kitchen table and I began to show the potential sellers my presentation using my iPad®, within minutes into the presentation the sellers quickly confirmed that they wanted me to list their property. From there I began completing the paperwork on my iPad®, and they signed electronically. My first outing with a visual presentation was a home run! The home sold and I earned a nice commission check, all due to this presentation. It was a great feeling, and a good wake-up call for me to learn how important it is to have a visual presentation when working with buyers and sellers.

Why Use a Presentation?

Why do presentations work? First and foremost, a lot of individuals learn visually. People are characterized as visual, kinesthetic, and auditory learners. Understanding how people learn is helpful when explaining your benefits and services. Because it is almost impossible to know what type of learner a prospect is when you prepare a presentation, it is best to try to cover all areas. To cover all aspects of learners, one option is to provide a visual and audio presentation along with touchscreen prompts or mouse clicking, in order to answer questions on a slide, with links to the answers provided on the PowerPoint®. To integrate the kinesthetic component, you could present similar printouts in a colorful folder with reference images and bullet points that the prospects can refer to during your meeting or during their leisure time. Or, if you want to go completely paperless, you can send the PowerPoint® to them as an attachment to click through and refer to later. (This is of course if you would like to leave your presentation with the prospective client. Some agents are against this. I will address the pros and cons later in this chapter.)

A visual presentation allows you to cover your points and handle objections in a more effective manner, versus trying to confront this and having your prospects retain everything you present from a verbal delivery. After all, people want to know what you plan to do for them as a real estate professional. If you've taken the time to create a personalized presentation for each individual customer, the rewards and the results can be phenomenal.

> "If you've taken the time to create a presentation, and even a presentation that could be easily personalized for each individual customer, the rewards and the results can be phenomenal."

I am not advocating for you to go through every specific slide in your presentation when meeting with customers and clients. I hardly ever go through my entire presentation with the customer. However, the various slides and information are available for me to address when I hear an objection, or there's a question about a specific topic.

If the customer asks a question or there is an objection that I do not have a PowerPoint® slide to visually explain, then upon returning to the office, I make up a visual for that question. For example, many times consumers may want to know if you can charge less for your commission. To include a slide that shows all of the various marketing efforts, work, and time you will be spending on their property helps justify your commission and why reducing your fee is not an option. You might also show how the total commission is shared between brokers and other agents involved in the transaction. Oftentimes consumers have no idea that your commission is split up and shared in various chunks with other agencies and agents.

Sometimes you may have a concern for specific types of marketing or advertising the client demands. Having visual examples available to the client helps to explain where your business comes from and why you use the marketing activities you use. This allows your client to better understand, in detail, your marketing process and, in turn, helps overcome any objections a client might have before they have them.

You may think that you can put together the perfect presentation. But trust me; others will have an objection or a new question about something you never thought about. Don't worry; you can always add that new information to your presentation slide deck. That is another great benefit to using digital technology. Additional information can be added at any time, and outdated information can be removed.

Format – Outline to Follow

In a course I concluded for my Masters of Real Estate Degree, we discussed this very topic, and why presentations are important for the real estate professional. My instructor provided a suggested outline for the class to use when preparing our PowerPoint presentation. Below is a recap of the outline/format Dr. Weinstein provided to our group:

- **Background Summary**

    Agent's background and expertise

    Company overview: What business are you in? (What needs does your business meet in the marketplace?)

    Purpose

    Mission statement

- **Assess Agent's Strengths**

    Agent's strengths

    Company's strengths

    Strengths of your property or services

    Pricing strengths

    Environmental factors that increase the value of your products or services

- **Real Estate Target Market Analysis**

    What is the market opportunity?

    What is the market size?

    What is the demographic makeup of the market?

    What are the key industry trends that are fueling your success?

- **Strategies of Your Marketing Mix**

- How does your marketing mix stand out from your competitors'? These should match the goals and objectives set by the agent or company.

    Product strategy (both property and services)

    Pricing strategy

    Place (distribution) strategy

    Promotional strategy

- **Identify Your Business Team and Membership**

- Include how your education, expertise, business partners, and organizations aid you in fulfilling the needs and wants of clients.

    Credentials

    Business organizations

    Realtor associations

- **Products or Services**

- Identify the best services you provide at the present time.

    Identify how your products and services fulfill a need in your target market. If you have more than one market you serve, explain the need for each target audience.

    Describe the features associated with your products and services.

    What methods are used to deliver your products and services?

    How do you differentiate yourself from your competitors?

    What can you do so that you better meet the needs of your clients?

    What new products or services would your clients most like you to offer?

- **Messages**

    What is the single best impression that you want your clients and partners to take away after each interaction with your company?

- **Conclusion**

    Summarize your key points and add contact information or a short biography.[1]

How Many Presentations?

Sometimes people ask me if they should have various presentations for various types of prospecting. My answer is always the same; it's your decision. There's nothing wrong with having a

---

[1]Weinstein, Margo, REALTOR® University Course, Real Estate Marketing Tools and Practices, 2015

specific presentation for expired listings, while another presentation might focus on the for-sale-by-owner. Both presentations and both types of sellers have different needs. Remember, the expired listing consumer is probably discouraged about their home not selling. They may even be discouraged with their previous agent or company. It's your job to help present information on what you plan to do, and how you and your company are different. Show them some of the marketing strategies you offer that your competitors in your marketplace do not. For example, perhaps you spend extra money to have an exclusive showcase-listing box through an online listing portal. Each time a consumer types in a specific zip code or city name (the zip code or city you subscribe to for this service), your active listings are displayed at the top of the web page, providing excellent exposure to potential buyers searching for properties in the local market you plan to advertise. Having a front and center promotional display can increase more potential buyers to the property. Trying to explain this verbally would not have much of an impact. Showing the consumer an example of how this page displays visually will again help tell your story in a powerful and positive way.

Keep in mind that you may also want to include some of the same PowerPoint slides with the for-sale-by-owner consumer. This is one reason I suggest you create one master PowerPoint presentation where you can have all of your slides grouped together. In that one master presentation, plan to cover all of the various points of interest about you and your company. You can then break the presentation into small chunks or pieces that are personalized for the prospective client, such as comparable listings in the area if you believe that a price change is in order to sell the property, or even just to show how long properties are typically on the market in that area. By creating one large master presentation with all of your potential slides, and smaller mini-presentations focused on a particular topic or interest, you will be prepared for any situation that arises. Remember that you can always pull up the master presentation and simply go to the specific slide or the slide number where it begins to talk about a topic that you need to visit during your presentation. Or you could use the mini presentation for the specific type of property or presentation that is needed.

I strongly encourage you to take the time and create a presentation that you can use when working with potential buyers and sellers. Yes, you need to prepare a buyers' presentation on why they should work with you as a buyer's agent. Buyers' needs are different from sellers' needs in a real estate transaction, and the information and slides are totally different.

Don't worry if you do not own an iPad® or some other tablet device on which to show your presentation to potential customers or clients. You can always print your presentation out on paper. You can also go to your local office supply store and buy a presentation binder for as little as twelve or fourteen dollars and create your own presentation manually. The most important thing to note, whether you choose presenting your information digitally or on paper, is to make it as professional and polished as possible.

I personally use an iPad® with an application that allows me to highlight and make notes, which is very effective while I'm in the field. Still, you can do this with pen and paper just as easily. The point to remember is that a presentation for buyers and sellers is a critical marketing piece that will help you win business and showcase you and your company's skills and talents. All of these points help to define how you are different from the competition.

Should You Leave Your Presentation With the Customer?

There are many schools of thought on whether you should leave your presentation behind with the potential customer who has not agreed to list with you. Some coaches and sales associates will tell you that it is not a good idea to leave your presentation behind for the competition to potentially have access to. If your presentation were to end up in the wrong hands, they may be able to tailor their strategic marketing plan toward your information. I use the other school of thought, where I do leave the information with the potential customer and do not worry about my report ending up in the competition's hands. My philosophy is to go in and do the best job I can, and deliver a winning presentation.

I do not believe there is a right or wrong answer for leaving your presentation with someone who does not plan to list with you. I agree with those advocating to only leave your presentation with people who want to do business with you. Still, at the same time, you may not sell their property and they may choose to list with another agent in the future. If that happens, they still have your information, and they could still share the report with your competitor.

I don't want you to get too hung up on the details of whether you should leave your presentation behind or not. My goal for this chapter is to encourage you to use a presentation aid when meeting with customers and clients. You should check with your broker or office manager to get their input on whether you should leave your information behind or not. Follow your broker's advice or whatever your company policy is regarding this subject.

Where Do You Begin?

The first step in preparing your presentation should begin with your office manager, owner, or broker. If you are an agent in a large organization, your training manager or director of

education may be able to provide the needed data. Find out what some of the marketing activities are that your company provides. Some brokerages actually produce professional videos that the agents are encouraged to integrate into their presentations that demonstrate the strengths and offerings of that brokerage. Spend time talking to other agents about what your company offers. Discover how long the company has been in business and any other historical information that is fitting to mention. How many top agents does your company have in the local board MLS? Does your office provide in-depth agent training for new agents after pre-licensed real estate school? Do you have any other certifications or designations you can include with your presentation? The average number of days your company's listings are on the market versus the average days on the market for your competition is also good to include. What's the average list price to sales price ratio for your office compared to the competition's ratios in your marketplace? Most of this data should be available through your local MLS.

There is a wide variety of data and information you should look for to tell your story. Determine if the information is worthy to be included or not. Of course, you only want to use information that will be beneficial or will put your company or yourself in a positive light versus your competition.

You will also need to make certain you have an adequate company logo and a professional photograph of yourself, and then utilize the company colors and branding in your overall design to be included with your presentation. The branding and synergy of making your presentation match your company's brand is essential. If you do have a personal logo or slogan I would incorporate that into the presentation, but I would also have the company's logo and branding information included. In fact, if you do plan to leave the presentation behind, you will want to be certain that you are following all of the rules and regulations of your state real estate license laws for advertising purposes. Someone may construe this to be a marketing or advertising piece if left behind, and you definitely want to abide by any real estate rules, regulations, or license laws pertaining to advertising.

If you are working with a franchise, chances are they already have a presentation template that you can use that includes the brand, colors, logo, and other information. Many franchises will also have various templates for buyers or sellers, complete with sample pages you can include. However, take the time to personalize any type of presentation template your company or franchise provides. Personalization to you and your business is important!

You should also take the time to put together as many slides as you can about why you and your real estate organization are the customer's final destination for their real estate needs. Again, you are building a master presentation file (a story) about you and your firm.

I would also strongly encourage you to include within the presentation what you plan to do for your potential client. What is your promise to the consumer? How are you different in the servicing of your real estate clients, or what are you proud of when you describe and explain the benefits of working with you? Remember that the presentation should not be all about how great you and your company are. Yes, you want to show the differences and what your company has accomplished through its history, but you also want to solve the customers' problems, and address their needs. Why do they want to work with you? What are you going to do for them? Don't forget to address the customers' needs and show how you can attempt to help solve any problems they may have, when building your visual presentations.

> **"Don't forget to address the customers' needs and show how you can attempt to help solve any problems they may have when building your visual presentations."**

You may not have to use your presentation on every listing or buying appointment. Sometimes, customers or past customers will call you to list their property, and there is really no need for you to go through your presentation. I've done business with friends. They know me, and they want me to list their property, so a visual presentation is a moot point.

On occasion you may point out a few things that you plan to do for your customers by using various sections of your presentation. But again, if they are short on time, and you do not feel a need to go over the presentation in detail, it's no problem. The main goal is to have a presentation ready when working with for-sale-by-owners, expired listings, future buyers, and other general prospecting appointments. It is also important to deliver the presentation thoroughly but efficiently, being sensitive to your client's time schedule.

I believe that you can win more business and be more effective versus the agent who chooses not to include a presentation. In my long history as a real estate broker and instructor, I can say with confidence that many of your competitors in your marketplace are not using presentation aids in their real estate businesses. By creating good presentations, you will definitely be one step in front of the competition. Available as a supplement to this book is a sample PowerPoint presentation that I use for sales.

Chapter 7

Introduction to **Prospecting**

If you want to have a successful real estate career, prospecting is vital. Without good solid leads that you can rely on for buyers and sellers, you will not go far in the real estate business. The following few chapters will discuss several prospecting solutions that you may consider with your daily activities:

- Building and working with your sphere of influence

- Developing a referral network

- For sale by owners (FSBO's)

- Expired listings

- Farming a geographical area

- Open house

- Direct mail

- Online marketing strategies

Why Prospecting?

Why is prospecting so important for the real estate professional? If you do not have buyers to work with or sellers to help sell their properties, then you will have no business to conduct as a real estate professional. Prospecting provides you the opportunity to find both buyers and sellers interested in your services. Keep in mind that prospecting may also help you to obtain referrals.

It is important that you create a daily prospecting plan to succeed. Unfortunately, most real estate agents will only prospect when they have little or no business. When their daily calendar fills up, they tend to put prospecting on the back burner. Having this seesaw approach to prospecting is not a good plan, and will lead to a business of highs and lows, driving many good agents away from the business. Remember this quote from the book if nothing else, *"prospecting must be done daily!"*

> **"Prospecting must be done daily."**

Prospecting is a numbers game. The hard-core reality about prospecting is that many people you approach will tell you "no." Whenever you hear the word no, or that your services are not needed, do not take it personally and be ready to move on to the next prospect. You are on the hunt, looking for that person who will say "yes, I need your services and I need your help." Don't give up, they are out there. If you manage your time wisely and devote a significant amount of efforts to prospecting daily, you will find new clients.

Your daily routine should include a time block for lead generation. It's important to note that not only should you spend time prospecting for new business, but you should also spend time nurturing your previous customers and clients, your sphere of influence, and others in your network. Let's examine how your prospecting schedule might look on a typical day.

8:00 AM – 9:30 AM	Review and respond to any previous emails, organize files, and follow up on missing documents, signatures needed, and other pending loose ends.
9:30 AM – 10:30 AM	Cold calling for new business, including expired listings, for-sale-by-owners, and others. This time block should be spent focusing on calling new business leads. During this time frame, you are looking for "new" business.
10:30 AM – 11:30 AM	During this time block, you should focus your attention on nurturing and "touching" your sphere of influence database. This is a good time to follow-up with past buyers to make certain everything is going okay for them, and to reach out to offer assistance or help. It's also an excellent time to ask if they know of someone who may be thinking about buying or selling.
11:30 AM – 12:00 PM	Follow-up on phone calls, check and respond to e-mail, file away documentation, and make notes from your two hours of prospecting.

Your afternoon should be spent with any appointments you have scheduled, your lunch plans, and of course any personal, business and family activities on your to-do list. You may be thinking to yourself, "But, John, you're living in a dream world. There's no way I can block out two hours per day to prospect." Yes, your mind is telling you there is no way, but if you truly put forth the effort, you can do this! In fact, just yesterday I attended a workshop offered by a good friend on the highly successful habits of real estate professionals. And he's discovered that high-producing agents put lead generation first and foremost every day. Prospecting is the life-blood of your business, and unless you prospect daily, you will not build a business that is high-producing and generating a profit. Without new leads, your pipeline will dry up and your business will be filled with ups and downs.

Also, don't make prospecting something to fear. How difficult is it to call a past client or customer and say the following:

"Hi David, it's John Mayfield. How are you doing? I know it's been a few months since we last talked, but I was thinking about you and Denise this past week and wanted to make certain everything was going okay

with your new home. How are Denise and the kids? How's your job? Did your daughter graduate from college? I know the last time we visited she was close to earning her degree. Also, David, if you hear of someone in the market needing to buy or sell real estate, please give them my name and phone number. Better yet, call me with their name and phone number. Perhaps you could help introduce me to them. As you know, my business is built on referrals and recommendations I receive from people like you. Thanks for your time. Let's get together in the near future for lunch or a cup of coffee.

Your follow-up phone call does not have to be long, drawn out or complicated. Touching base, asking how their real estate transaction is doing, checking on family, their job, and what interests and hobbies they have shows that you care, and keeps your real estate career front and center to your sphere of influence. If you're thinking to yourself, *I just don't feel comfortable calling this person*, then remove him or her from your list. It's important to only keep prospects on your list that you feel comfortable calling. I will help explain building your list whom you can include, and various ways to contact these prospects in the next chapter. For now, just remember, if you do not feel comfortable prospecting to a particular person, then remove that individual from your list.

For new prospects, the script is much different. Explain who you are, identify yourself as a real estate professional, ask a few questions, and then request an appointment to visit in person with the customer. Here's an example of a very successful script I use when calling for-sale-by-owner listings.

Hi, my name is John Mayfield, with Mayfield Real Estate in Farmington, MO. I noticed you have a house for sale on 1412 Anystreet. I would like to know how much you are asking for your house. How many bedrooms does your house have? Is there a basement? By the way, is it possible for me to take a quick look at your house? I promise I won't need much time, and I also promise that I will not be there to try to sell you on my services. I like to look at all of the inventory in my area of specialty, and it's good for me to know what is available in case I have a customer or client who might have an interest in your house. When is a good time for you, and what works best for your schedule?

Using that script, I can generate an appointment 99 percent of the time. And when I arrive at the home, I focus on being brief, refraining from selling, and establishing a relationship with the customer. It's the follow-up that will help me win the business. I'll discuss this concept more in the "Working For-Sale-By-Owners (FSBO's)" chapter.

If you plan to prospect for expired or for sale by owners, there are many good letters and marketing ideas you might consider. I have provided a few examples at the conclusion of this chapter that have been successful for me.

Don't underestimate the need to prospect via your social media networks. Many real estate agents are using Facebook, LinkedIn® professional networking services, Twitter and other social media sources as good ways to keep in touch with their friends and contacts. A simple comment on a Facebook friend's photo or post can be a good way to keep your name in the prospect's mind. Also, when you do use Facebook or another social media platform, do so with sincerity and generosity. It will not profit you to simply focus on your sphere of influence, with meaningless and bogus comments continuously in their social media feeds. When you reach out through one of these mediums, do so with sincerity.

Speaking of electronic prospecting, remember to use social media platforms like Facebook and LinkedIn® to post, comment and participate in groups. Taking an interest in reading the group threads is an excellent way to learn new content. I also helps build positive relationships. Simply helping another group member on LinkedIn® opened up an opportunity for a paid speaking engagement for me, where I spoke to a group of real estate professionals in Warsaw, Poland, all expenses paid. Again, I received this business opportunity because I used social media to network and participate. Through networking, you could actually say I was prospecting, and this form of prospecting paid off!

Finally, I am reminded of two of my older real estate mentors who have since passed away, but both gentlemen taught me a valuable lesson about prospecting that still works today: Get out and meet people! My two mentors were constantly visiting small business owners, the local coffee shops, and other interesting places around our local community. Why? Because getting out in the trenches and talking to the movers and shakers in your area can produce a wide variety of good leads. As my teacher in college would often remind us, you need good "bird dogs" helping to lead you to business. There is nothing wrong with attending your local chamber of commerce meetings, Rotary, Lions, Optimists, Toastmasters and other groups for networking with business leaders in your community. I even secured many good leads and closed a lot of real estate transactions by joining both a bowling and golf league. Remember, networking is a form of prospecting, and developing relationships through participation in groups or visiting businesses and friends around town will offer you profitable results.

Now that you understand that prospecting is a major part of developing your career, and you are committed to prospecting daily (understanding that many folks may say no), you are well on your way to jumpstarting your real estate career. The following chapters provide detailed information, solutions, and ideas for winning new business through various prospecting methods.

Chapter 8

Your Secret Tool,
Your Sphere of Influence

Your Sphere of Influence

Your greatest opportunity for jumpstarting your real estate career is to focus and concentrate on your sphere of influence. This is sometimes referred to as your center of influence. Stephen Covey coined the phrase "raving fans." Whatever terminology you agree upon for naming these folks, you should know this is your greatest asset and your secret tool for use as a real estate professional.

Where Do You Begin?

For the purpose of this text, we will refer to this prospecting category as your sphere of influence, (S.O.I.). This list of individuals (S.O.I.) should consist of between 100 and 400 contacts. In Ben Sherwood's book, *The Survivors Club*, he informs us that the average person knows approximately 300 people on a first name basis. According to Sherwood's math, the average person is then only two degrees of separation from 90,000 contacts! Don't panic. I'm not suggesting that you must build a list of 90,000 contacts, but hopefully you can quickly understand the need for developing an S.O.I. of the people you know and building friendships. In reality, you should consider a targeted list of anywhere between 150 to 400 close friends and acquaintances.

How should one go about preparing a list of contacts? My main suggestion would be to construct a list of people you know who can help provide business to you. Remember, not everyone on your S.O.I. will have real estate needs in the future. However, these contacts will know others who may have immediate real estate needs. Therefore, it is important to have your sphere of influence always on the hunt to refer real estate leads and business to you.

Suggested S.O.I. Format

I have a method that has proven successful in building a S.O.I list. First, make a list of everyone you know in your marketplace. Everyone! During this first pass, don't worry about whether you know them well of not. If you can think of their names, then add them to your list. Think about individuals you have done business with, worked for or with, attended worship services with, volunteered at organizations with attended school activities and civic functions with, etc. Yes, it should be a HUGE list!

Once you have this master list in place, it's time for you to reduce your list to a manageable group of names. There is no minimum number of core fans to include with your list, but you should finalize the group to 100 or more names if possible. These names are people you do not have a problem calling and folks you will regularly contact to help you build your real estate business.

You may hear others encourage you to add as many people to your list as possible. Coaches and mentors will vary, but at the end of the day it's your decision to add them or not. I recommend that you include the names of those you will possibly stay in touch with on a regular basis.

I like to combine both approaches into one sphere of influence database. First, you want to try to develop a list of as many people as possible. Again, hopefully you will have somewhere in the neighborhood of 300 to 400 potential acquaintances you can include with this list. Once you have the initial database in place, you will learn to work this list in two ways, as described in the next section.

The 80/20 Rule

In the 1930s, an economist by the name of Vilfredo Pareto noted that eighty percent of Italy's land belonged to twenty percent of the population. This observation was later coined the *Pareto Principle* by management consultant Joseph M. Juran. It is a fascinating concept, and one that is surprisingly accurate.[1]

When examining and comparing the *Pareto Principle* to various organizations, it's easy to witness its truth. For example, many organizations typically receive the bulk of their help from a small fraction of the members. Donations from church members fall into the twenty percentile of those who financially support its cause. Even a small percentage of sales associates produce the bulk of your business in your office. In fact, research your local MLS or your office and find out who the top earners are and how much sales volume they produced last year. Chances are you will discover that only twenty percent of the sales associates provided most of the business for your company or through the MLS as a whole.

How can you as a real estate professional use the *Pareto Principle* with your sphere of influence? First, you can begin to go through your list, separating the individuals into either the eighty percent group or the twenty percent group. For simplicity sake and to help you remember this concept, label your twenty percent group as the "A" category. After all, they are your best leads and source for business. If you wish to make a good grade in school, you would want to earn an A, so why not label this group as the A's. I have provided an illustration below of how you could label a category. The balance of the folks in your database will receive a "B" label.

Title	Name	Address	City	State	Zip	EMail	Phone	Category A-B-C

Who do you put into each category, and how do you determine which person or contact in your database becomes labeled as either an "A" or a "B"? It's quite easy, and here is how I want you to

---

[1] Wikipedia - http://en.wikipedia.org/wiki/Pareto_principle, March 27, 2015.

think about segregating your list. First, if you have someone you would take to lunch, then label him or her an "A." If you have no problem inviting this contact to play golf or attend a show, then he or she needs to be categorized as an "A."

Examine the names on your list and ask yourself if you would feel a little awkward calling this contact and inviting him or her out to a business luncheon. Even though you knew this person and included them on your S.O.I. list, if you feel a little awkward inviting them for lunch or another type of event, then they probably need to be either removed altogether, or labeled a "B." Remember, you don't want to throw away this business or discount these contacts from ever sending you a lead. But at the same time, these folks would probably not be worthy to be classified as an "A," or within your twenty percent group.

You should also go through your master list and throw out any contacts you believe are not worthy to be on either your "A" or "B" list. If you would feel awkward or out of place corresponding with these folks throughout the year, then you should remove them from your database. It does not mean you could not come back and add them later, but for the interim, you should label and place them in your "C" category.

Scrub Your List

It is now time to do a second run-through with your database of names. Look back through the list and ask yourself, upon reviewing each contact, if anyone on the list is a mover or shaker in your community. Perhaps they hold a prominent role in some community organization or your place of worship. Does their job put them in contact with people who are moving in and out of the community regularly? Examples of these types of connections might be school principals, teachers, superintendents, human resource managers, etc. If you quickly recognize someone who falls into this section who is in one of these roles, I would encourage you to label them as an "A" contact.

Preparing your list will be a challenging and difficult task, but spending time over the next few weeks to do so is necessary. I encourage you to prepare a printout of your database and carry it with you or have it electronically with you for timely updating. While you are out and about working in the community, you will think of individuals you should include as part of your S.O.I., and meet new folks to add to the list. In fact, a good friend of mine refers to his S.O.I. as his "met" database. If you meet someone, then you need to stay in touch with him or her. That's why I like to refer to your database as a living and breathing project, requiring you to fine-tune, update, and categorize it often.

Building a good Sphere of Influence list is your first priority to building a successful real estate career. You need to build a list of names and contacts that will help contribute leads and referrals for you. Take the time to ensure that you have categorized and constructed an excellent database.

Experienced Agents and Your S.O.I.

As an experienced real estate agent, you should take time to go through past transactions and make certain you have included your past clients and customers. Consider adding both closed transactions and even expired listings. Yes, even if you did not produce a buyer for these past customers, include them on your list. Even buyers you were unsuccessful in finding a home for, or buyers who pulled out of the home purchasing process while working with you, should be on your list. Any potential customer or client you have collaborated with throughout your real estate career should be considered for your S.O.I.

Don't let this exercise discourage you. After all, many past clients and customers may have been overlooked or neglected. Some may not have received any correspondence or communication from you for months or even years. It's okay. You're moving forward, and the past is behind you. Naturally, some of these contacts may have transacted business with another agent, or maybe you have no desire to communicate with a few of these people. Still, there may be several contacts you may have missed as you research and study your past clients and customers list.

Possible Ways to Build Your List

As noted earlier, this process may take several weeks to complete. One suggestion you might consider for building your S.O.I. is to drive around your local community, recording names and street addresses on a digital recorder. As you drive through neighborhoods, you may recall friends who live in these areas who should be added to your list. You might also look through membership directories, think about parents and friends of your children, consider people at your bank, and more. All of these actions allow you the opportunity to grow your S.O.I.

The 30/15 Rule

Your plan is to contact your sphere of influence on what I label the 30/15 approach. Your "A" contacts (twenty percent group) will receive a touch from you thirty times throughout the calendar year. Your "B" contacts (remember these are the eighty percent in your S.O.I.) will receive a touch fifteen times throughout the year. A "touch" is any communication with the contact. Whether it is a phone call, email, personal visit or direct mail, you will classify this as a touch. As you move through this chapter, I will provide you with a broad variety of marketing suggestions that you may consider implementing in your real estate business.

Many times marketing suggestions or activities might be used for both "A" and "B" marketing activities. However, if one approach might be more suited for a particular category, such as your "B" group, then use that type of marketing for only one group.

Let's go back to the *Pareto Principle* for a moment. If his research and conclusions are correct, then twenty percent of the people within your database will provide you with the bulk of your business or referrals. At a bare minimum, you need to reach out to these people thirty times throughout the year. I know that seems overwhelming, but it can be done, especially through many of the marketing tactics I have provided in the book. Don't forget; these are the movers and shakers, and your good friends!

However, you don't want to discount your B group, as these contacts can offer a wealth of leads for your business, too. You might consider sending these contacts a monthly newsletter or postcard a few times a year, along with a phone call or handwritten note. But they do not need to be contacted as often as your A group. Again, the goal for your "B" group is to contact them fifteen times throughout the year.

It is important for you to remember that from the author's research, and the statistics and data provided by the National Association of REALTORS®, the biggest part of your business (and business from other real estate professionals) is generated from referrals and recommendations by friends, family members, and coworkers.

I am a technology person, and I live and breathe tech gadgets and real estate. However, I do firmly believe that an address book is essential. Having the ability to add names and addresses of new contacts, including updating email addresses and phone numbers of your sphere of influence, is essential to your success. Your database is your gold mine. It is your book of business! If you learn to take your address book with you wherever you go, you will be able to add names to your database when you meet people. Having the ability to add folks you failed to include on your list, or fix errors and make changes, as discovered, is important. Get in the habit of asking your contacts for their current phone and email information when you're out in the field. Add new contacts and business as they develop throughout the year. Carrying a hard copy address book with you will provide many advantages. Of course, you will want to go back and change or add any new information to your computerized database. (I will provide some resources at the conclusion of this chapter for possible CRM (Contact Relationship Management) software solutions you can use with your real estate database).

I suggest that when you add new people to your computerized database that you have recorded in your paper address book that you take a yellow highlighter and highlight their names. This will ensure that each record has also been added to your computer database. For example, if you are out in the field and meet one of your contacts that is in your database, and you learn they have a new phone number, you can list the change in your book, then transfer it to your computer database. Once the change is completed in your computer database, you can highlight the change in your book. This will alert you that the change has been updated in your computerized database. If there is no yellow highlighted notation in your book, then you need to update your other records with the new changes.

These are suggestions and possible solutions for you to consider for keeping track of your S.O.I. At the end of the day, you should use what works best for you. Many real estate agents use their smartphone as their CRM and database of contacts. This might not be the best system for you to consider, especially as your business grows. I would encourage you to make sure your computerized CRM syncs with your smartphone. In fact, you might use your smartphone as your resource for updating your S.O.I. when you are in the field and discover new updates and changes that are needed.

Recall from our research that the majority of real estate agents can barely pay their monthly bills. I believe you should begin your practice differently from the average real estate professional. For those of you who are experienced and have purchased this book because you want to jumpstart your real estate career, it's time you do something different. Remember the Chinese proverb, *"If you are doing the same thing over and over expecting different results you surely will go insane."*

Hopefully this chapter has helped provide a vision for your real estate business, and why you need to develop a good sphere of influence database. It is important for you to spend the majority of your daily prospecting contacting and following up with people included in your S.O.I. **Your S.O.I. will provide you the greatest return for your business. I believe it is also the quickest way to success as a real estate professional.**

As promised, I am providing several links and resources to some electronic databases you might consider. Remember that companies change from time to time and may merge or change their website. If a web link is broken or you cannot find the company, skip over that one. There's also some sample letters you might consider using to send to your sphere of influence.

If you have an interest in more letters like those featured, visit all of the "5 Minutes" books for real estate agents at OnCourse Learning, Amazon, or my website, http://www.BusinessTechGuy.com.

www.TopProducer.com

www.boomtownroi.com

www.zoho.com/realestatecrm

www.contactually.com

www.realtyjuggler.com

www.realateiq.com

www.propertybase.com

www.insiderrealestate.com

[Date]

Address Block

Greeting Line

I am excited to announce my affiliation with *[Agency Name]* in *[City]*, *[State]*. After successfully completing my educational requirements and passing the state real estate exam, I am now ready to serve you with your real estate needs. *[Agency Name]* offers a continuous and detailed training program for their new agents to assure their clients and customers the same quality service others have come to expect.

I want you to be aware of a couple of key points about the real estate industry:

- According to a recent survey by The National Association of REALTORS®, most buyers found their real estate agents by recommendations from a family member, neighbor, or friend.

- The real estate industry normally pays agents on commission sales. In other words, I am paid only if I am involved in a real estate transaction with a buyer or seller.

- Referrals from you are a key ingredient to the growth of my business!

I hope you will think of me if you know of someone interested in buying or selling real estate. Please give that person my name and phone number, or feel free to call me with the name and phone number so I can make the first contact. Your help will play an integral role in my development as a real estate professional!

Thank you for your help, *[Letter Name]*, and I appreciate your friendship and support.

Sincerely,

[Agent Name]
[Agent Title]

From "Five Minutes to a Great Real Estate Letter" – OnCourse Learning

[Date]

«AddressBlock»

«GreetingLine»

I thought you might like to know about the latest sales figures from [City] or [Neighborhood or Subdivision]. Below is a brief explanation for the average sales price, number of days a typical home is on the market from list date to sale date, and the percentage of list price to sales price.

City	Number Sold	Average Sales Price	Days on Market	% of List to Sales Price

My goal is to provide this information to you quarterly; however, feel free to contact me any time you would like to know this information, and I will gladly provide it for you.

I appreciate your time, and I hope you will think of me if you know of someone interested in buying or selling real estate. Please give that person my name and phone number or feel free to call me with the name and phone number so I can make the first contact. Your help will play an integral role in my development as a real estate professional!

Thank you for your support, [Letter Name].

Sincerely,

[Agent Name]
[Agent Title]

From "5 Minutes to a Great Real Estate Letter" – OnCourse Learning

[Date]

«AddressBlock»

«GreetingLine»

I thought you might like to know about the latest sales figures from *[City]* or *[Neighborhood or Subdivision]*. Below is a brief explanation for the average sales price, number of days a typical home is on the market from list date to sale date, and the percentage of list price to sales price.

Number Sold	Average Sales Price	Days on Market	% of List to Sales Price

My goal is to provide this information to you quarterly; however, feel free to contact me any time you would like to know this information, and I will gladly provide it for you.

I appreciate your time, and I hope you will think of me if you know of someone interested in buying or selling real estate. Please give that person my name and phone number or feel free to call me with the name and phone number so I can make the first contact. Your help will play an integral role in my development as a real estate professional!

Thank you for your support *[Letter Name]*.

Sincerely,

[Agent Name]
[Agent Title]

From "5 Minutes to a Great Real Estate Letter" – OnCourse Learning

[Date]

«AddressBlock»

«GreetingLine»

The busy buying-and-selling real estate season is here, and I am now accepting new clients! That's right! If you know of someone in the market to buy or sell a home, I can help.

Now is a great time to buy or sell a home, and I am in a good position to devote my experience and time to new buyers and sellers. I would appreciate your recommendation to anyone you know interested in buying or selling a home. Thank you!

I hope all is well with you, *[Client's Name]*, and I thank you for your time.

Sincerely,

[Agent Name]
[Agent Title]

From "5 Minutes to a Great Real Estate Letter"– OnCourse Learning

[Date]

«AddressBlock»

«GreetingLine»

Wanted! Buyers and sellers, any price range, any location!

Sometimes I would like to be that blunt with my advertising, but I know it wouldn't be effective in my marketplace. One great reason I do not have to resort to that kind of advertising is because of a good referral base from my friends and family. Thank you!

Right now my inventory is low. Most of my current buyers have found homes to buy, and my current listings have sold. It's good news, but for a real estate professional like myself it also means my business will begin to slow down if I do not restore my inventory of buyers and sellers. If you know of someone in the market to buy or sell real estate, please let that person know about me.

I hope all is well with you and your family, and I appreciate your continued support with my real estate career. Thanks again for your referrals!

Sincerely,

[Agent Name]
[Agent Title]

From "5 Minutes to a Great Real Estate Letter" – OnCourse Learning

[Date]

«AddressBlock»

«GreetingLine»

It's great to see green grass and flowers in blossom, and to hear birds singing again, not to mention the increase in real estate bustle at our office. Spring is always an enjoyable time of the year for many people. I hope you're having a great month and enjoying this season change too!

I wanted to write and remind you of how my success in real estate is dependent on referrals from friends like you. Do you know of someone considering buying or selling? If so, please let that person know of my services. Many agents (including myself) appreciate and value the referrals sent to us from our friends and family members. Thank you for always promoting my name when you hear of someone thinking about buying or selling real estate.

I appreciate your time, *[Letter Name]*, and if you need help with any real estate needs yourself, remember I am only a phone call away.

Sincerely,

[Agent Name]
[Agent Title]

From "5 Minutes to a Great Real Estate Letter" – OnCourse Learning

[Date]

«AddressBlock»

«GreetingLine»

I hope you're having a great year! Summer is here, and the real estate market is still going strong. Don't forget; if you know of someone considering buying or selling, be sure to give that person my name. I love referrals, and these leads from friends like you are critical to my business success.

I appreciate your time, *[Letter Name]*, and if you need help with any real estate needs yourself, remember I am only a phone call away. I hope this year continues to bring much happiness to you and your family, and again, thank you for your support!

Sincerely,

[Agent Name]
[Agent Title]

From "5 Minutes to a Great Real Estate Letter" – OnCourse Learning

[Date]

«AddressBlock»

«GreetingLine»

I hope you're having a great year, and I hope you're enjoying this wonderful change of season. Our real estate market is still strong, and I'm looking forward to a great third quarter in real estate sales.

Don't forget; if you know of someone considering buying or selling real estate, be sure to give that person my name. I love referrals, and these leads that friends like you provide are critical to my business success.

I appreciate your time, *[Letter Name]*, and don't forget, if you need help with any real estate needs, I'm only a phone call away.

As always, thank you for your support!

Sincerely,

[Agent Name]
[Agent Title]

From "5 Minutes to a Great Real Estate Letter" – OnCourse Learning

[Date]

«AddressBlock»

«GreetingLine»

Odd as it may seem, winter is often an excellent time to sell real estate! Why? Generally, there is still a good supply of buyers looking for real estate but a smaller number of properties to choose from. These conditions make what we sometimes refer to as a "seller's market." Unfortunately, many sellers take their real estate off the market until springtime, thinking this is the best time to sell. True, spring is an excellent time to list real estate, but the competition is much greater, allowing buyers more to choose from.

If you know of someone considering a move soon, please remind that person of my services. The success of my career is dependent on referrals from friends like you, and despite what many people may claim, now is a great time to buy or sell real estate!

I appreciate your time, *[Letter Name]*, and thanks in advance for always remembering me when you think of real estate.

Sincerely,

[Agent Name]
[Agent Title]

From "5 Minutes to a Great Real Estate Letter" – OnCourse Learning

Chapter 9

Developing a Referral Network
That Pays BIG Dividends

Building a Referral Network

Existing real estate agents understand that referrals are a major part of success for many real estate professionals. Creating a referral game plan for your sphere of influence (recommendations from your raving fans) is the strategy I would like to discuss in this chapter. Although this method may only be used once, twice, or a few times per year, it can be an effective program for generating long-term consistent results. As a disclaimer, some of the information shared in this chapter may not be applicable for your location. However, reading the information will hopefully generate an idea or two that you can use within your real estate business.

Types of Referral Programs

Let's talk about several different types of referral programs you might consider implementing in your real estate business. First, we've already discussed your sphere of influence (S.O.I.) or raving fans. They could include former coworkers from another profession, family members, friends and others. The goal of your S.O.I is to communicate with them regularly. For example, the 80/20 rule (A and B contacts) and the 30/15 method, as detailed in the last chapter. Relying on the Pareto Principle, we will contact our twenty percent a minimum of thirty times throughout the year. Our "B" contacts will receive a touch approximately fifteen times during the calendar year. The theory behind this principle is that you should work the smaller (more profitable) group more often, as the bulk of your leads will come from twenty percent of your database–the A contacts!

Local Small Business Database

The second type of database I want you to focus on is a database of local business professionals in your community. You want to make certain the people who are listed in this particular database are not also included with your sphere of influence database.

This specific referral database of small businesses that I am suggesting is for the local businesses (small business professionals) that live in or around your community. In fact, I would encourage you to include as many small business owners as possible. One way you can build this list is by joining the local Chamber of Commerce. Sometimes your local chamber will provide a list of other members of the Chamber of Commerce for you. If you are fortunate to have this luxury, you can easily download or copy the list to a software program to use with your direct mail marketing. If you do not have access to a computerized list, you can always take the time to manually add these individuals one by one. As with your S.O.I., this will require a lot of work, and the database (like the S.O.I.) is an ever-changing process. However, over time, you will have a valuable resource of possible referral leads if you invest in building this small business database.

I would also encourage you to include the following when building this local area small business database:

- Owner's name

- Business name

- Mailing address

- Phone number

- Email address

- Website address

Add specific notes about the business for your database. For example, where is the business located? How long have they been in business? What is the main product or service they supply? Do you know others who have used their business or services? The more information you have about this business in your database, the more beneficial it will be to you.

Your goal for your new business S.O.I. database is to communicate with the owners about what is happening throughout the year in your real estate community. This might be an annual report, semiannual update, or even a quarterly mail out to this specific database. The goal behind this referral program is to make the local businesses aware of who you are, and how the real estate market is performing in your local economy.

Understand that mailing information is one piece of this business S.O.I., but a critical step in this referral program is building relationships. You should attempt to stop in some of the small businesses and visit with the storeowners or managers from time to time. Make a quick introduction, exchange business cards, and let them know about the future correspondence you plan to provide. If it's a restaurant, have lunch there sometime. Remember, your next client could come from your local coffee shop or drycleaner.

Online Business S.O.I. Marketing Strategies

If you're a real estate professional who wants to add social media, blogging, video, and other online Internet marketing strategies, you might consider doing a short interview for a podcast or blog post about the company. Perhaps you can make this a video interview with the owner, touring the premises and giving a hearty thumbs-up for consumers to check out this business.

People like to do business with people they like and with those who do business with them. If you appear to help their business they may remember to do the same for yours.

I want to stress that this type of referral system is an ongoing, living and breathing business plan!

> "Remember, a referral system is an ongoing, living and breathing business plan!"

You will need to update and refine your business S.O.I. database regularly. Also, don't believe that you have to create this database overnight. It may take several months before you will be ready to begin sending out information to this list. Your goal is to develop relationships and build a valuable database of resourceful business friends you can exchange referrals with throughout the year.

Long-Term Results of a Business S.O.I.

Let's think about the long-term effects this type of marketing program should have on your real estate business. Remember, you're targeting small business owners in your community. Now consider where possible relocating consumers will visit or go when they arrive in your marketplace. Chances are they'll be staying at a local hotel, visiting a small grocery store or convenience store, and dining at several local restaurants. People new to an area may also want to ask the small business owners questions about the community to find out more information. I'm sure they want to ask questions about schools, recreational activities, dining, shopping, and more. And yes, nine chances out of ten, the conversation may turn to real estate. By developing relationships and communicating with the local small businesses in your area, you will position yourself as the go-to real estate person with this database. Think about the number of referrals you may generate if you nurture and develop this business S.O.I database correctly!

There are countless other reasons why you should consider a small business referral marketing program. Some business owners may be thinking about selling property themselves in the near future. Many of the small business owners have regular customers who come in to shop regularly and have developed relationships and friendships with these individuals. This will put the small business owner with firsthand knowledge before anyone else when the customer is planning to sell, upgrade or relocate out of the area.

Having small business owners and managers of local stores on your team recommending and referring you for real estate business is a no-brainer. And besides the benefits already mentioned, consider the companies on your list who may be hiring new employees to work at their businesses, especially employees relocating from outside the area. Chances are you will be the first real estate professional with the inside lead and access to such individuals for their real estate needs.

Database of Real Estate Agents Outside Your Marketplace

Another excellent source of real estate leads (overlooked by many real estate professionals) is communicating with agents and agencies outside your local marketplace.

> **Another excellent source of real estate leads (overlooked by many real estate professionals) is communicating with agents and agencies outside your local marketplace.**

For example, my company is close to St. Louis, Missouri. Farmington is approximately one hour south of St. Louis. Because our community is considered a commuter town, many families and individuals want to relocate to Farmington. Moving their families to a rural setting for more outdoor activities is attractive to consumers, not to mention the lower property prices. A big bulk of my business comes from real estate agents who know me from the St. Louis marketplace. Granted, I have had many of these referring agents in real estate training courses I have taught in St. Louis, still, the referrals happened because I took the time to build relationships with the referring agents.

Many of the leads have come through my friends and affiliations through the state Association of REALTORS®. I'm also aware of various agents who come down to list property or show property in my area. Rather than fearing these agents as competitors, these are the perfect individuals to get to know and develop business relationships with. Consider targeting these agents and sending correspondence, encouraging them to refer their business to you, instead of wasting their valuable time driving so far to show or list property.

If you take the time to communicate with agents outside your marketplace, you may find them giving you business when they do not have time to travel for business inquiries they receive. For example, I have one good friend in the St. Louis market who has referred several prospects to me. She has also recommended me to numerous agents within her firm because of our affiliation and friendship. Even though the agent you may communicate with and send information to throughout the year may not have a referral for you, they may know another agent in their office who might possibly have a potential client in your area.

This list does not have to be extensive, and should not be a time-consuming process. Throughout the year, begin adding names of other agents you meet at conferences, or who list and sell occasional properties in your area. For example, if you notice a for sale sign with an out-of-town real estate agent in your marketplace, reach out to that person and get to know them. Give them your contact information, and offer to help show the property to any potential leads they may get in the future. Most agencies will offer a compensation split, and of course you could negotiate a fair referral fee from any leads they may give you. Consider an agent who has a sign in your marketplace that lives one hour or even thirty minutes away. Naturally, interested buyers who like the listed property's exterior appearance may call about this property or look it up online. If they like the information about the property and the price sounds right, they may want to schedule an appointment to preview the inside. If the out-of-town listing agent is busy or not able to drive the required distance, you may be the agent they turn to for help, because you reached out and created a relationship with the out-of-town real estate competitor.

Building Your Out-of-Area Agent Database

How do you go about building this type of database? As noted earlier, keep an eye out for agents who are active in your marketplace and live some distance away. Remember, as real estate agents and companies, we must adhere to all Anti-Trust laws! There can be no price fixing or no business restrictions to specific areas. I'm not trying to encourage any Anti-trust violations, but there's nothing wrong with telling someone that you're available to help them if they have a showing requested and it conflicts with their schedule. It's also a good idea to offer to look at the property the next time the agent is in your area. This will allow you to begin building a business relationship/rapport with the out-of-town agent, plus familiarize yourself with the property.

Second, you should reach out to some of the larger offices in and around your area–preferably those larger offices that are thirty to sixty miles away. Try to find out who the top agents are in these companies, and send introductory emails to them. Introduce yourself and explain your passion and desire to assist them with any potential referrals they may have in your marketplace. You might also consider reaching out to the branch managers of some of the larger offices. The managers normally receive requests from their agents asking whom they may know in your area when they have a referral for your marketplace.

Third, you should expand your search to the top companies or areas throughout your state. After all, many folks relocate from within the state they reside in. If you are an agent in a warmer climate or an area where there's a lot of relocation business coming from other areas, consider targeting agents or companies in those cities. For example, Florida, Arizona, California, or Texas agents might look at building relationships with agents and agencies in Chicago, New York, Boston, or Minneapolis.

As with any S.O.I. database, you must think long-term when working the out-of-area agents prospecting method. Creating any type of database with leads and contacts is not something that you build overnight. In fact, your first or second mailings may only consist of a handful of names. Still, as time goes by and you research and record the activity of what's happening in your marketplace where the specific leads are coming from, you will build a valuable and profitable referral database program from other agents.

Human Resource Managers Database

Another referral activity database you should consider is a human resources or (HR) database. This database may or may not work for your area. However, if you live in a community where there are many small industries, hospitals, or other corporations with many employees, then you're in luck!

This database will consist of those individuals who hire (and sometimes terminate) employees. Many small to large manufacturing facilities and corporations in your marketplace normally have an HR person on staff. You might also consider including school superintendents and principals on this specific database list. Communicating to individuals who hire new employees, especially employees relocating to your area, is important.

What do HR folks want to know from you, the local real estate professional? Try to put yourself in their shoes as an HR professional. If you were hiring new recruits—job applicants whom you may be trying to persuade to pack up their belongings and come work for your company—what would you want to know from the local real estate professional?-What about the potential new employee who needs to encourage their family and children to move across the state or even the country? What do you think one of the questions might be during their interview with the HR person in your area? How are the new housing stats? Are there local sports teams for children? Do concerts/theatrical performances come through town? The local HR person has a keen interest in knowing what is going on in your marketplace. Helping these individuals know what's going on in the real estate market may help provide you with an opportunity to work with a potential candidate interviewing with the firm or hospital. There are many excellent reports you can print and share with these HR contacts from your local MLS or through the REALTORS® Property Resource (RPR) network. Consider mailing a monthly or quarterly report to these individuals, and as with any type of database of contacts, nurture and build your business relationships over time. In addition to sending reports, you may also clip out articles and other interesting news and information about the area. Show you care about your marketplace and that you have the experience and expertise to handle their new recruits with professionalism.

Commercial Brokers and Property Managers

Commercial brokers and property managers normally like to work and stay in their own particular field. After all, commercial brokers know the commercial industry and are best suited for those types of properties. I am more of a residential person and a small acreage and farm broker. Even though I know a lot about commercial activity and have attended several CCIM (Certified Commercial Institute Managers) courses, I do not have the expertise to effectively market commercial properties. Considering this disconnect between residential and commercial, communicating and fostering relationships with commercial real estate practitioners can be advantageous for potential future referrals. Get to know some of the commercial brokers and property managers in your area. As with your other S.O.I leads, add them to your database and send them your real estate activity reports and information throughout the year. You'll be surprised at the potential referrals and business these folks can send you, especially when residential customers and clients ask them for advice or recommendations.

I know you are probably wondering why I would encourage you to have four or five separate databases. The reality is you do not have to have different or specific databases for each of these groups. You can have one database, tagging or specifying with some type of labeling system within your database software how this person should be categorized. For example, when you want to send a specific market update or correspondence to human resource managers, you'll be able to do so by selecting the appropriate tag when you mail merge your list.

Please note I am not suggesting or recommending that you communicate with this database on a weekly or even monthly basis. Frankly, most of these people don't have time for too much correspondence from you. However, a quarterly postcard or semi-annual update of what's taking place in the residential marketplace is a nice gesture and a piece of information that they may want to know about and share with their colleagues or potential candidates moving to the area.

I would also encourage you to specifically focus on information that would be meaningful and practical to these specific groups. Human resource managers probably want to know if the real estate market is either going up or down. They may also want to know the average sales price for your area, and what kind of homes and properties potential candidates can get for their money. Providing this type of information or data is absolutely priceless for building relationships.

The same could be said for small business owners. They may be more interested in demographics and other types of sales data. Think about providing reports and articles that are beneficial for them and their businesses. For example, sharing small business ideas or how someone else is profiting from a marketing or technology system could be something you could share with these folks. Even providing step-by-step instructions on how to reach more customers using video or social media might be attractive topics for this specific piece of your database.

Agents outside your marketplace may not be concerned about what's going on in your area, but they might be interested in knowing more information about you and perhaps sales-related tools that have been profitable for your company or other top agents in your marketplace. Try to create something of value for agents who live outside the area, but at the same time highlight why you are the go-to person for referrals in your area.

You do not have to communicate each and every month to these types of groups. This is a nurturing process. However, these activities can pay big dividends if you farm and cultivate this database two to three times per year.

> **"Remember, referrals are the lifeblood of the successful real estate agent."**

Remember, referrals are the lifeblood of the successful real estate agent. Consider and think about ways you can leverage contacts from other real estate agents outside your marketplace—from commercial brokers, small business owners, and human resource managers, to the leaders in your community who are movers and shakers. All of these connections may have possible referrals for your real estate business. By following some of the plans and steps in this chapter, you will be well on your way to jumpstarting your referral real estate business!

The balance of the pages in this chapter provides you with some sample letters you might consider using to send to your sphere of influence. If you have an interest in more letters like those featured, visit all of the "5 Minutes" books for real estate agents at OnCourse Learning, Amazon, or my website, http://www.BusinessTechGuy.com.

[Date]

Address Block

Greeting Line

Thank you for the recent referral you provided me. I appreciate your help and support with my business, and yes, referrals are an important part of my continued success in the real estate industry. Please know that I will give *[Client's Name]* the utmost care and professionalism with *[his/her]* real estate transaction.

Again, thank you for the referral *[Letter Name]*.

Sincerely,

[Agent Name]
[Agent Title]

From "5 Minutes to a Great Real Estate Letter" – OnCourse Learning

[Date]

Greeting Line

Address Block

Just a note to let you know that I recently closed with *[Clients' Name]* on their real estate transaction and to again say thank you for the referral! I appreciate your help and support with my business. Referrals are such an important part of my continued success in the real estate industry, and it's people like you, *[Letter Name],* who help make this all possible.

Again, thank you for the referral!

Sincerely,

[Agent Name]
[Agent Title]

From "Five Minutes to a Great Real Estate Letter" – OnCourse Learning

Chapter 10

Working **For-Sale-By-Owners** (FSBO's)

Working For-Sale-by-Owner Properties

Probably one of the most rewarding prospecting methods that I have used throughout my real estate career has been through prospecting for-sale-by-owners. Yes, it can be a little overwhelming at first, but the end results can often be financially fulfilling.

Before we begin exploring some possible ideas and marketing strategies for setting up a for-sale-by-owner prospecting plan, I want to tell you why I continue to have success calling on for-sale-by-owners today.

Around 1981, when I was in my early twenties and having good success with my real estate career, I had the opportunity to attend a sales training program in St. Louis, Missouri. The topic for that particular day of training was on working with for-sale-by-owners. At the time, my parents and I had purchased a Better Homes & Gardens real estate franchise. The training course for this particular day cost a whopping twenty-five dollars. My parents, who were running the real estate brokerage, had encouraged all of the sales associates to attend this sales training event. Several of my colleagues had signed up to attend. However, when I arrived in our office parking lot to meet the other prospective attendees, no one showed up. I was discouraged because St. Louis was a little over an hour away, and I was wondering if I should go ahead and attend this program by myself. The thought of walking into a training program with other agents from around the area whom I probably did not know was a little intimidating. Nevertheless, I decided to make the trek to St. Louis and attend the workshop. What I learned that day from the seminar literally changed my real estate career! I can honestly say that the techniques, methods, and plans I put in place after attending that for-sale-by-owner program launched my real estate career into overdrive.

Why was this one-day event so successful for me? First and foremost, it's an easy-to-follow program. Second, it's not pushy, and I am not a pushy salesperson. Third, it's a no-brainer! I'll get to the no-brainer part a little bit later, and I'm sure you, too, will agree that calling on for-sale-by-owners is a prospecting method that will definitely help you jumpstart your real estate career in five minutes or less!

The Roger Searcy Plan

Here's what the instructor taught us that day about the for-sale-by-owner program. His name was Roger Searcy. If you know Roger, please be sure to tell him I still talk about his for-sale-by-owner workshop some thirty years later. To Roger, I say thank you!

Roger taught us a simple and basic for-sale-by-owner prospecting action plan. First, you call the prospect and introduce yourself. Always identify yourself as being a real estate associate. Next, ask a few basic questions about the property, and then you immediately ask the consumer if you can come by and take a quick look at their home. (Please refer to Chapter 7, "Introduction to Prospecting" for my for-sale-by-owner script).

I'm sure I scared many of you away by that bit of information. However, remind yourself that the person doing a for-sale-by-owner listing wants to sell their property, at least we hope they do. If not, then they probably are not a viable prospect, and you should scratch them off your list and move on to the next potential possibility. I can honestly tell you that I have spent a large portion of my thirty-six-plus years in real estate, using Roger Searcy's for-sale-by-owner method, and I have only had one or two people ask me why I wanted to see their home. If they ask you why you would like to view their home, or become mean or arrogant in any way, then scratch them off your list! After all, they are probably not worth meeting, and you don't need to work with those types of people. I believe it's important that you continue to concentrate on customers and potential clients who will indeed be serious about buying or selling real estate, in addition to people you enjoy working with.

The second step in this for-sale-by-owner strategy is to then arrange an appointment. When they agree (ninety-nine percent of the time they will say yes), tell the consumer that you need to check your appointment book and see what time you have open. Understand that most consumers want to work with people who are busy, so avoid saying you have nothing going on now, and can come right over. Use a script, and always check to see when your next opening is available.

Once you set the appointment, arrive on time, greet the customers, and begin the preview of the home. I would encourage you to ask a few questions, perhaps regarding their current marketing activities and other information about the property. Don't spend too much time at the home and try to avoid asking for the opportunity to list the property. This first meeting needs to be informal, laid-back, and nonthreatening. Use a comfortable approach with the consumer. Granted, there have been times when I have toured the property for the first time and walked away with a a listing forty-five minutes to an hour later. But don't feel like the purpose of the first meeting is to list the property.

The third step, prior to leaving the property, is to ask the consumer if anyone has ever provided them with a comparative market analysis, sometimes referred to as a CMA. By offering a free price evaluation, you provide yourself an opportunity to have a second meeting with the for-sale-by-owner. It also enables you to put together a marketing plan for the potential client. While using this approach, approximately ninety-nine percent of the conumers agree to the free CMA and allow me the opportunity to meet with them for a second time.

Step four is a crucial part of the success of this for-sale-by-owner prospecting program. As soon as you arrive back at your office, sit down and write a thank you card, and place it in the mail to the potential sellers. Again, this is probably one of the most important steps in the entire program!

Naturally, to heighten your chances of success with the for-sale-by-owner you need to look professional and act professional. If you can do this, and avoid coming off too pushy, you will be on your way to securing a new listing. Trust me; it works most of the time!

Providing a sincere and genuine handwritten note, thanking them for allowing you the opportunity to visit with them regarding their real estate needs is a definite winner.

> **"Providing a sincere and genuine handwritten note, thanking them for allowing you the opportunity to visit with them regarding their real estate needs is a definite winner."**

I emphasize sincere, as I do believe you should write this card as though you mean it. Showing your appreciation and thankfulness for the opportunity to come out and visit with them is important. A large percentage of the people I meet regarding for-sale-by-owner activities have been so kind and nice to me that we became good friends though our business relationship. Again, I am thankful they were nice to me, and allowed me the opportunity to look at their property, so the thank you card is sent out of sincere appreciation.

There are some interesting apps for your smart phone that allow you to take a photo of the house, type a thank-you note on your smartphone, and press the send button. The customer will receive a glossy postcard within two to three business days. Postagram is my favorite app to use for implementing this marketing idea, but some other options are Touchnote and Ink Cards. Ink Cards is actually a greeting card instead of a post card, if you would prefer a more formal approach. All of these options typically run under two dollars per card. The timeliness of the delivery is important due to the fact that I'm hoping that my second follow-up visit will be within one to two days from our initial meeting. It is important that my thank you card arrives before my next visit, when I present my CMA findings.

Your Comparative Market Analysis

If the FSBO agrees to have you prepare a CMA, be sure to produce a good quality comparative market analysis for the for-sale-by-owner. There are many good programs available. Realty Tools©, Cloud CMA©, and Top Producer© are a few of the companies specializing in robust CMA software systems. However, technology vendors tend to come and go, so be sure to use your favorite search engine provider to look for real estate CMA software companies for a complete listing of products and businesses. You can also use your MLS as your research and report format. For members of the National Association of REALTORS®, the new REALTORS® Property Resource (RPR) is a wonderful CMA report. This program will offer many local market statistics and several other illustrations you can give to the consumer.

Once your report is prepared and your presentation is available, you should be ready for your second appointment. Here you will provide the presentation, visit more with the FSBO, and discuss any marketing ideas or questions they might have regarding your presentation.

Before you leave, encourage the sellers to reach out to you if they need additional help with marketing the property, or have other questions. Sometimes I will offer to help look at an offer that might come in from a potential buyer, or encourage helping with writing ad copy or even preparing a sample for-sale-by-owner flyer template. Recently, I suggested to some folks to use my RPR report and share it with any potential buyers, showing them my evaluation of their property and the price I recommended for their home. Not much time had elapsed before they asked me to come out and list their property because they were tired of trying to sell their home themselves.

Ask if the sellers have any additional questions, and then go ahead and leave the appointment without being too pushy or overselling with the potential client. Many of the for-sale-by-owners I call upon will often list with me during the second interview. Again, I am not trying to close the listing at this time, but I am asking a few questions or testing the waters to see if they may be ready to put the property for sale on the market. But it's always best to be prepared to sign the prospects if they are ready to list.

Your next phase is to simply stay in touch through cards, letters, and phone calls. Periodically stay in touch with the customers until you can win the listing or they choose to list with another agency. If you build a relationship, stay in touch, and do not come off as being too pushy, I believe you will win the listing.

Many times for-sale-by-owners will tell me that they have a good friend in the business or a family member who sells real estate part-time. Some will even inform me that they go to a specific House of Worship with a friend that they probably will list with if they do plan to go that route. I still follow my same for-sale-by-owner game plan, offering the free CMA, asking for the second follow-up appointment, as well as staying in touch. Everyone knows a real estate agent, but how many smart, hard-working, energetic agents do they know?

Remember, some sellers do not want to do business with close friends or family members. Sometimes if this person they know is not very active, I have even worked out a referral fee for that friend so they were still involved in the transaction but allowed someone like myself (a full-time professional) to handle the transaction. The key is following up and staying in touch with the for-sale-by-owner.

> **"The key is following up and staying in touch with the for-sale-by-owner."**

By following this game plan, I have secured and won more business from this for-sale-by-owner prospecting method. As I noted earlier, it really is a no-brainer if approached properly. After all, most sellers want to sell their real estate. Some need to sell, and over time, they will get tired of trying to sell their property on their own. The person who stays in touch, develops a friendship, and communicates the value they can bring to the table will normally win the business!

Now let's get started and take a look at some sample ideas and suggestions you can incorporate to win the for-sale-by-owner prospecting method to jumpstart your real estate career in five minutes!

The balance of the pages in this chapter provides you with some sample letters you might consider sending to your sphere of influence. If you have an interest in more letters like those featured, visit all of the "5 Minutes" books for real estate agents at OnCourse Learning, Amazon, or my website, http://www.BusinessTechGuy.com.

[Date]

Address Block

Greeting Line

I hope you had a chance to review the information I left at your house recently, and I trust you found it helpful. I understand your preference to sell your property on your own, and, to help you with this, I am making available a video called *Preparing Your Home For Show*, by David Knox Productions, that you can borrow. This is an excellent program that points out information you should know and steps to complete to help get top dollar for your property.

I would also like to offer you an opportunity for a free price evaluation on your property to help you find out what it's worth on today's real estate market.

To borrow the video or receive the FREE price evaluation, call me, *[Agent's Name]*, at *[Phone Number]*. There is no pressure or obligation to list or sell through me or my company.

Again, thanks for your time, and please call me if I can help in any way.

Sincerely,

[Agent Name]
[Agent Title]

From "5 Minutes to a Great Real Estate Letter" – OnCourse Learning

[Date]

Address Block

Greeting Line

I hope you had a chance to review the information I left at your house recently, and I trust you found it helpful. According to the *2003 National Association of REALTORS® Profile of Home Buyers and Sellers*, the biggest concern among for-sale-by-owners is completing the paperwork. True, there is an enormous amount of forms that need to be completed to make the transaction run smoothly. This includes everything from the seller's disclosure statement to lead-based paint addenda to occupancy before and after the closing provisions and, of course, the contract itself.

I understand your desire to sell your property on your own and respect your decision to do so. To help you with this endeavor, I am making available to you sample copies of some of our forms for your attorney to look at and incorporate in your transaction. Unfortunately, I cannot provide you with free forms since our contracts come from our REALTORS® association. However, you are more than welcome to borrow my sample packet if your attorney would like to incorporate some of the same information in his or her sales contract. Let me know if you would like to see this, and I will be glad to drop it by.

I would also like to offer you a price evaluation on your property to determine what it's worth on today's real estate market. This does not take long, and many of my clients find this information helpful during their own marketing efforts.

To use my sample forms packet or receive your price evaluation, call me, *[Agent's Name]*, at *[phone number]*. Best of all, they're both FREE, and there is no pressure or duty to list or sell through me or my company.

Again, thanks for your time, and please call me if I can help in any way.

Sincerely,

[Agent Name]
[Agent Title]

From "5 Minutes to a Great Real Estate Letter" – OnCourse Learning

[Date]

Address Block

Greeting Line

Thank you for allowing me to visit with you about the real estate you are selling on your own. I appreciate your kindness and the hospitality, and I wish you the best of luck on your home sale. I have enclosed another business card if you should have any questions during your marketing efforts. Please feel free to call me if you have a concern or question that you would like to discuss.

I have enclosed a sample seller's disclosure (marked **Sample**). You should discuss this form with your attorney before providing it to potential prospects and before entering into a written offer to purchase. Unfortunately, I cannot provide you with a copy of this seller disclosure since this form is for our office transactions only. However, your attorney should be able to prepare a similar document for you to use.

Again, thanks for being so kind and generous during my visit. Good luck, and please let me know if I can help in any way.

Sincerely,

[Agent Name]
[Agent Title]

From "5-Minutes to a Great Real Estate Letter" – OnCourse Learning

[Date]

Address Block

Greeting Line

I want you to know that I still want to help you market your property if you are interested in doing so. I have enclosed some more information for you to look over. Please give me a call if you need further explanation on this information.

You have a lovely house, and I enjoyed our visit when I was out there. As I mentioned before, thank you for allowing me the opportunity to meet with you about your real estate needs. Please let me know if I can help.

Sincerely,

[Agent Name]
[Agent Title]

From "5 Minutes to a Great Real Estate Letter" – OnCourse Learning

Chapter 11

The Secret to
Working Expired Listings

One profitable area for jumpstarting your real estate career is expired listings. There are several good reasons for working this particular real estate segment. Specifically, the expired seller understands how the real estate listing process works. When you think about the expired listing customer for just a moment and what they have been through over the past three to six months (or longer), you can appreciate their patience and tolerance while waiting to sell their home.

Reasons This Is a Good Prospecting Arena

Let's list a few reasons why this particular group would be an important prospecting portfolio to consider. First, as noted previously, the expired listing customer understands how the entire listing process operates. After all, they have had their property listed for sale and experienced the highs and lows of having their property toured by buyers. Some expired sellers even experience zero showings. Perhaps the expired seller never even had a follow-up phone call or report from his or her agent. Yes, believe it or not, lack of communication is a commonly noted frustration by many sellers. And these are just a few of the trials and tribulations most expired listing sellers faced during their listing period. So if this particular customer still has an interest in selling their property, then they are probably motivated and perhaps ready to adjust their asking price.

Second, the expired listing consumer is probably more open and palatable to entertain a price reduction. Many of the expired listings that I take have incurred big price adjustments, placing the property in the marketplace at a more realistic price.

> "The expired listing consumer is probably more open and palatable to entertain a price reduction."

Third, the expired listing consumer is normally tired. My wife and I recently purchased a new automobile, and we had looked for several months at various cars through numerous auto dealerships. Quite frankly, it was an excruciating process, and we eventually wore down. Yes, we became tired of the whole process! When we finally found the car we both liked, my negotiating skills and my attempt to purchase the car at a lower price had diminished. We purchased the car, and as I pulled away from the parking lot I realized I probably could have done a little better at negotiating the purchase. However, we were ready to make the purchase and were a little tired of all of the car shopping. We both wanted to end the process. The same happens with most expired listing customers. If they want to sell, then they want to end the process. Many finally realize they cannot get the asking price they originally hoped for, and others just want to get their lives back to normal. Price reductions and motivated sellers are common traits you will discover when working with expired customers.

Another positive reason for calling on the expired listing consumer is the ability to create a presentation and a marketing plan that will say, "Wow!" After all, the expired listing customer probably did not have a pleasant experience, so if you get the opportunity to show them a marketing plan with pizzazz, you will be one step in front of your competition.

If you plan to prospect in this category, you must have an effective and dazzling marketing program that you can share with consumers. In other words, most consumers who allow their property to expire and do not resign with the same firm are generally looking for someone who can do a better job. Not always, but as a general rule, the expired seller is looking for a fresh start. I realize that many times listings may show up expired, and the client is happy to re-list with their existing agent. It's just a matter of having the necessary paperwork signed and submitted to the MLS to appear active.

Other expired listing customers may decide to take their properties off the market. It's simply not part of the listing inventory from this point forward. They are tired and a bit discouraged, and they may decide not to sell at this time. This does not mean these folks will never come back to the marketplace, but perhaps they have changed their mind for a short period, and have no plans on re-listing in the near future.

Still, others are discouraged and unhappy with the office or agent they were with. These expired customers are looking for someone new! A real estate agent who is willing to roll up their sleeves and go out to try and find a buyer for their property is a dream come true for the expired listing customer. This is why it is so important to have an effective listing presentation and a marketing plan for an expired listing consumer. After all, if you can provide a detailed game plan on what you will do for this seller, they will be impressed and eager to give you an opportunity to sell their property. If that's the case, you need to execute and implement your marketing plan to the expired customer. And if you sell the property (quickly), you will be someone special in their eyes, earning referrals and repeat business for many years. And yes, these new clients and friends will be willing to provide you with some glowing testimonies about your service as a real estate professional!

As noted earlier, there are many advantages to calling on the expired consumer. They are familiar with the process, they are eager to sell, they are looking for someone who can work and provide some different alternatives, and they generally will lower their listing price to make the property more in line to where it should be priced for the local marketplace.

Disadvantages of Working Expired Listings

One of the disadvantages to calling expired listings is that it does require a bit of work and attention to detail. If you're randomly sending out one or two letters, you probably won't have a lot of success. Most real estate agents I know who do an excellent job recruiting expired consumers have a game plan. Their expired listing system will contact the customer over a period of weeks.

If you want to have success in the expired listing prospecting category, you need to set up a system of letters, postcards, and phone calls.

Another disadvantage to calling on expired listings is the feedback that some agents see in their local marketplace. Granted, any listing that expires in a multiple listing system and is not showing active is legally available for any real estate agent to prospect. Most state laws require you to identify yourself as a real estate agent, and of course you should also make certain you inquire as to whether the consumer is under an existing agency agreement with another agency in your area before calling the expired listing. When prospecting through direct mail, you should always provide a disclaimer, and make certain that you follow and adhere to all local real estate ordinances in your state or domicile.

Even if you adhere to all of the rules and regulations, and have verified that the listing has indeed expired and has not been re-listed with another firm, you may still encounter some drawback or negative consequences from other agents in your marketplace. Growing up as a real estate professional in my community, I was privileged to have a good relationship with many of the local agents. Even to this day, I have a good relationship with many of the other agents in my area. We work well together on cooperating transactions. With that said, sometimes I find it difficult to try to win an expired listing away from another agent or agency with whom I have a good relationship. After all, we work with these folks day in and day out on many various transactions throughout the year. If you are constantly prospecting the former customers and clients of other agents, you can sometimes create a bit of friction in your business relationships. Deciding whether you want to call on expired listings is a choice and decision that you will need to make on your own. I will caution that if you are trying to develop relationships with other agents throughout the local marketplace, remind yourself that this type of prospecting may not be palatable to some of the other real estate professionals in your marketplace. However, the expired listing prospecting tool can be a successful venture if you follow some of the guidelines and suggestions in this chapter. Be sure to fine-tune and adjust your program to what works well for you and your marketplace.

Final Note

One final note about prospecting expired listings. Each office will have their own rules and policies on whether you can call on expired listings that may have been listed with your real estate organization. Make sure you find out the policy your office has for calling on expired listings previously listed with your firm before you begin making sales calls. As a broker/owner, my policy was always to avoid other agents calling on expired listings my company once listed, unless the agents agreed that someone else could approach the past customer or client. Oftentimes I might have one agent in my office that did not work well with a particular client, and I would allow a new agent to assist or work with their old client. Normally, both agents would agree upon some compensation or referral split that would be satisfactory to them both. My philosophy was that I did not want to have agents directly competing or calling upon other agents' clients in my office unless they had agreed upon this in advance.

To begin our exploration of creating an expired listing program, it might be good to take a look at one or two specific types of correspondence that can be used when prospecting the expired listing. I've included a letter for those readers who belong to the National Association of REALTORS®, and have access to the REALTORS® Property Resource (RPR). The letter on the next page provides an example of this RPR expired listing letter.

Have You Heard About The New "RPR" Pricing Model?

It's very accurate and FREE to all of my Customers

As I was searching through our multiple listing service (MLS) today, I noticed your house had recently expired. I am sure you understand that since your listing has expired it is no longer available to potential homebuyers through the MLS website, REALTOR.com, and many other online listing portals. Don't get discouraged because your property did not sell; it might just indicate that you need a fresh, new beginning to jumpstart your marketing activity.

I am now using the <u>NEW</u> *"RPR"* (*REALTORS® Property Resource*) Appraisal Model to accurately help my clients and customers know exactly what their property might sell for. It's absolutely FREE, and it's amazingly accurate!

I also offer a wide variety of innovative marketing ideas to help sell properties quickly. I have over 36 years of experience and a wide array of marketing ideas I would love to share with you.

Please feel free to call me at 573-756-0077 to set up your FREE consultation on how we can get the most for your property, and to receive your FREE *"RPR"* Price Opinion on just what your property is worth on today's market.

Thanks for your time, and I hope to hear from you soon.

Regards,
John D. Mayfield, [ABR, CRB, e-PRO, GRI]
Broker/Author/Speaker

Please void this offer if your property is currently listed with another real estate broker.

As noted earlier, to have an effective expired listing program, you must go further than one letter to the customer. I would suggest following up with a second piece of correspondence, either a postcard or another letter. Keep in mind: prior to sending the second letter, you should make certain that the property has not been re-listed with the previous agency or another agent in your MLS. You will also want to provide a disclaimer on each and every correspondence that tells the customer to avoid the message or to please excuse your communication if they have re-listed or listed their real estate with another real estate agency. I would suggest sending the next piece of correspondence within seven days from your first letter. It is also a good idea to include a mix of phone calls with your follow-up program. As with the FSBO program I shared in the previous chapter, feel free to use the same script and process for obtaining an appointment with the expired listing customer. Remember, the key to winning the expired listing is consistency! Don't send one letter and quit. Keep the follow-up program on a full-court press, and you will jumpstart your real estate career in five minutes.

The balance of the pages in this chapter provides you with some sample letters you might consider using to send to your sphere of influence. If you have an interest in more letters like those featured, visit all of the "5 Minutes" books for real estate agents at Oncourse Learning, Amazon, or my website, http://www.BusinessTechGuy.com.

[Date]

Addresss Block

Greeting Line

Hi, my name is *[Agent's Name]*, and I noticed your listing has recently expired from our multiple listing service (MLS). Unfortunately, this means that your property does not appear in any computer searches other real estate agents use when working with potential buyers in your price range.

If you're still interested in selling your property, I would love to visit with you and explain some of my marketing ideas that have been successful for many of my clients. I have enclosed a sample flyer and a postcard that I use in my marketing campaigns for new listings.

If I can help in any way, please give me a call. I hope to hear from you soon.

Sincerely,

[Agent Name]
[Agent Title]

Please void this offer if your property is currently listed with another real estate broker.

From "5 Minutes to a Great Real Estate Letter" – OnCourse Learning

[Date]

Address Block

Greeting Line

Hi, my name is *[Agent's Name]*, and I noticed your real estate listing has recently expired from our multiple listing service (MLS). Unfortunately, this means that your property will not appear in any computer searches other real estate agents use when working with potential buyers in your price range.

May I ask you two questions?

☐ *Are you still interested in selling your real estate?*

☐ *Do you feel a fresh start with another real estate agency might be helpful in selling your home?*

If you checked either box above, then perhaps I could help jump-start your marketing efforts for the coming weeks. I would love to visit with you and show you some of the marketing strategies I use in selling properties.

For this FREE, no-obligation consultation, please call me today. I appreciate your time, and I hope to hear from you soon.

Sincerely,

[Agent Name]
[Agent Title]

Please void this offer if your property is currently listed with another real estate broker.

From "5 Minutes to a Great Real Estate Letter" – OnCourse Learning

[Date]

Address Block

Greeting Line

Hi, my name is *[Agent's Name]*. I noticed you had your house for sale recently, and I was wondering if you are still interested in selling. I have a unique marketing plan I would love to share with you, as well as some other ideas I feel will help to sell your property.

Now is a great time to buy and sell a home! For a **FREE** price evaluation on what your property is worth on today's real estate market, call me at *[Agent's phone number]*. There is no pressure, or contract to buy or sell through me, and the entire process does not take long.

I appreciate your time, and I hope to hear from you soon.

Yours truly,

[Agent Name]
[Agent Title]

Please void this offer if your property is currently listed with another real estate broker.

From "5 Minutes to a Great Real Estate Letter" – OnCourse Learning

[Date]

Address Block

Greeting Line

Hi, my name is *[Agent's Name]*. I realize your house did not sell while listed through our Multiple Listing Service, but don't let this discourage you; there may be a good reason. Sometimes a fresh start with a different real estate company makes all the difference in the world. I would love to visit with you and explain some marketing ideas I use, as well as give you my feedback on what would help to sell your house.

Call me at *[Agent's phone number]* if this sounds like something you're interested in. Please understand there is no obligation to buy or sell through me. I promise not to take up much of your time and, yes, it is absolutely FREE!

I appreciate your time, and I hope to hear from you soon.

Sincerely,

[Agent Name]
[Agent Title]

Please void this offer if your property is currently listed with another real estate broker.

From "5 Minutes to a Great Real Estate Letter" – OnCourse Learning

Chapter 12

Farming a **Geographical Area**

Creating a Farm Area

Another type of prospecting I've always enjoyed is referred to as farming a particular area of your community. Normally, a farm area will consist of a subdivision or other geographical boundaries that you determine for soliciting consumers about their real estate needs. Farming can be a fruitful and profitable prospecting method when performed correctly.

A farm area should consist of anywhere from 100 to 500 homes. I have seen agents who farm a much larger area than this, but to be effective you should focus on a number and size of homes you feel confident you can handle.

There are many ways to develop your database and list for this farm area, depending on your location and the information available to you. Some agents in larger markets have the ability to pull tax records and download other key information about consumers in the farm area, along with mailing addresses and other important information about the properties.

Unfortunately, some real estate agents (like myself) live in rural areas where a farm area may need to be cultivated and developed manually. There's nothing wrong with getting to know your farm prospects and consumers by using the old-fashioned method for developing your database.

As with your other prospecting and databases for referral networks, and your center of influence, creating a database for your farm area is important. After all, you will be mailing information to the farm area regularly. You will also need to visit your farm area in person from time to time. Because of your various types of communication to your farm area, I suggest you keep your farm area to a number that you can adequately and consistently work.

> "As with your other prospecting and databases for referral networks, and your center of influence, creating a database for your farm area is important."

Why Have a Farm Area?

Why is farming effective for the real estate professional? First, it allows you to begin building relationships with those who live in your farm area. Keep in mind that many of the people who live in a specific geographic area that you farm may have real estate needs in the near future. They may also know family members, coworkers, or friends who are getting ready to buy or sell real estate in your local marketplace. They might even know folks in other states or areas who want to buy or sell real estate! If you position yourself correctly as the go-to real estate professional in your farm area, you may be able to earn out-of-state referrals directly from your farm area.

Second, your farm area customers would like to know what is going on in their subdivision or community. After all, wouldn't you like to know what your home might be worth if you lived in the subdivision and you were not actively involved in the real estate business? There are several examples I will provide that will help you win business in your farm area, and I'm sure you will come up with additional ideas and suggestions from your broker and other agents in your office over time. The important point to remember is that you want to build a relationship in your farm area. You also want to provide your farm area with activity and information on what is happening in their local marketplace. Granted, I have heard of agents who have put together subdivision directories, newsletters, and tips on home repairs, recipes, and much more when communicating with a farm area. Still, at the end of the day, I believe most people are curious as to what housing prices are doing in their location or subdivision. Making decisions about real estate is usually one of the largest financial decisions most consumers will make in their lifetimes. Helping consumers to understand what's going on in the marketplace, and how their financial investment is performing is a huge opportunity for you to assist consumers.

To recap, the first step is to select the geographic or specific subdivision that you want to work as a farm area. I normally encourage real estate agents to look at the multiple listing activities and determine where a good region or subdivision might exist. In other words, you want to pick a subdivision that is active in sales and properties that are relatively easy to sell. Therefore, you should spend some time researching and investigating the subdivision you want to begin farming. Keep in mind there may be other agents farming in this location; however, don't let the old adage "everyone else is doing that" scare you off and away from farming a busy and vibrant subdivision. Remember, you are armed with determination and skills.

Get Your Farm Area Approved

I strongly encourage you to discuss the farm area with your branch manager, owner, or executive broker in your office. Sometimes offices will assign specific farm areas to agents in your company. Your office may even have a policy in place to avoid doubling up in an area or allowing additional agents to prospect in the same locations. Be sure to get their approval and discuss with them whether they believe this location will be profitable for you to farm as a real estate professional.

Build Your Database

Once you've chosen the location you plan to farm, your next step is to build a database of the consumers who live within this farm area. Be sure to include the following in your farm database:

- Name

- Mailing address

- Phone number (if possible)

- EMail address

- Any other information that you might want to track.

Depending on your CRM program, you can include other notes such as the number of times the home has been sold or listed in the past, has expired or foreclosed, and any other activities about the home. Remember, like many of the other prospecting methods in this book, it may take time and hard work to develop an effective and beneficial database. And once this information is in place, you will be able to begin working your location and reaping the benefits.

If you can download the information noted from a local tax record system, MLS, or other portal in your area, I would strongly encourage you to do that first. More than likely you will then need to go in and clean up the records, pulling out the information that is meaningful and deleting the data or tax information you will have no use for. After all, if you plan to do direct mailings, you want to be able to easily upload your list to an online postcard service or to your own printer. Check out expresscopy.com©, The Personal Marketing Company©, and VistaPrint©, to name a few. You can also use your favorite search engine to search for real estate postcards or flyers to find additional vendors specializing in this line of work. You can always change the font style to a handwritten font, and do some other clever marketing touches to make your direct mail pieces look attractive. For now, concentrate on building your database and obtaining the names and mailing addresses of each person in the farm area where you plan to work.

Be certain to look in the tax records for the owners' mailing addresses. Not all owners live in the properties or homes in the subdivision you will be farming. Some may live out of state, and when you are mailing correspondence or information to the owners, you want to make certain your direct marketing piece gets to the right individuals.

If you send a marketing flyer or postcard to the home address and the tenants or renters open the letter, it may never make it to the seller. These same tenants may in fact be late on their rent, and the seller could be dealing with one large headache. Therefore, always make sure your database has the legal owner's name and mailing address, as recorded at the courthouse.

> **"Always make sure your database has the legal owner's name and mailing address, as recorded at the courthouse."**

You can keep both addresses (property and mailing) in your database. The largest percentage will have the same addresses, but for your database purposes, keep two separate fields for each record. Note: you want to somehow actively identify in your database what the current property address is if the owners do, in fact, live out of the area, and whether the property is used as a rental or for other purposes.

Now that you've chosen your farm area and have had this location approved by your managing broker, it is time to begin corresponding with the consumers within your farm area.

A Marketing Plan for Your Farm Area

The following includes a few letters, postcards, and examples of information you might consider sending to your marketplace. Some of the information provided has been taken from previous 5-Minutes books that are available to purchase from OnCourse Learning Publishing.

[Date]

«Address Block»

«Greeting Line»

Did you know the average sale price for *[area]* is *[average sale price]*? That's right: according to our latest Multiple Listing Service statistics, the average sale price for a single family home in *[area]* is *[price]*. In addition to these findings, I have noted that it takes approximately *[number of average days on market]* days to sell a single family home in our community. I have enclosed a detailed report of average sale prices and days spent on the market for several types of properties in various areas of our community. I think this information may be of use to you for future reference should you, a family member, or a friend consider purchasing a home.

I hope all is well with you and your family. I appreciate your time, and I hope that I can be of service to you in the near future. Remember, if you know of anyone who may be interested in buying or selling a home, I would love to help them. Please pass along one of my business cards. I have enclosed several for you to hand out should a possible referral arise. Thanks again for your support with my real estate career, and I hope to hear from you soon.

Sincerely,

[Agent's Name]
[Agent's Title]

From "5 Minutes to Great Real Estate Marketing Ideas" – OnCourse Learning

[Date]

«*Address Block*»

«*Greeting Line*»

Selling Your Home Doesn't Have To Be That Difficult

If you've been frustrated or discouraged by the process of trying to sell your home, don't get too discouraged—I have several marketing techniques that I think can help you sell your property quickly. For a "FREE", no-pressure and no-obligation consultation and appointment to hear more about these marketing ideas, call me at *[agent's phone number]*. Feel *free* to check out my web site at *[agent's web address]* for some of the marketing techniques I'm employing for my clients.

Thank you for your time, and I hope to hear from you soon.

Sincerely,

[Agent's Name]
[Agent's Title]

From "5 Minutes to Great Real Estate Marketing Ideas" – OnCourse Learning

[Date]

«*Address Block*»

«*Greeting Line*»

Did you know?

Did you know your home is no longer for sale in our local Multiple Listing Service computer database? Since your listing has expired, your home is no longer available to potential buyers and real estate agents through our Multiple Listing Service. If you're still considering selling your property, I would love to visit with you about the marketing campaign I have designed for expired listings. I feel confident that you'll agree, after seeing this presentation and marketing campaign, that it would be beneficial for you. Sometimes a change of direction and a fresh breath of air is all an expired listing needs to sell quickly.

I have enclosed an article entitled *"5 Important Marketing Strategies That I'll Employ for You."* These are just a few of the many marketing ideas I have implemented for all of my listing clients. It's also available on my web site at *[agent's web address]*. You can reach me at *[agent's phone number]* to arrange an appointment to hear more about my marketing campaign. As always, thank you for your time, and I do hope to hear from you soon.

Sincerely,

[Agent's Name]
[Agent's Title]

From "5 Minutes to Great Real Estate Marketing Ideas" – OnCourse Learning

[Date]

«Address Block»

«Greeting Line»

Don't Just Take My Word on It

I know many times real estate agents talk a big game, but when it comes to delivering results, it can sometimes be a different scenario. Rather than explaining a little bit about my customer service in this letter, I thought it would be good to enclose some brief testimonies from my satisfied customers and clients. As you will see from these letters, my service and commitment to you go beyond the call of duty.

I do hope that you will give me an opportunity to visit with you about your real estate needs. You can reach me at *[agent's phone number]*. Thank you for your time, and I do hope to hear from you soon.

Sincerely,

[Agent's Name]
[Agent's Title]

From "5 Minutes to Great Real Estate Marketing Ideas" – OnCourse Learning

You might be wondering if farming a market or subdivision is worth the time, energy, and effort. And to that I have to say absolutely yes! First of all, don't make farming a subdivision too difficult. In the old days, before personal computers, fax machines, and any kind of computerized record-keeping system at the local courthouse, I was farming specific areas in my marketplace. I always liked to go out and knock on doors in my farm area, especially when the weather was bad or uncomfortable. My thought process was, if consumers see me knocking on doors as a real estate professional in inclement weather, they would remember my name and believe I was a hard-working real estate professional.

One snowy, frigid day, while knocking on doors in my farm area, I was handing out a small marketing piece. I had created a coupon and titled it "Free Market Analysis." Basically, I copied the coupon on white office paper, using the copy machine. The coupon entitled the recipient to a free price evaluation of their home's worth in the real estate market. Of course my contact information, photo, and other details were also on the coupon. I met many people on that cold day in my farm area as I handed out coupons. Many of the free offers were left in-between the storm door and the front door if no one was home.

After a day of knocking on doors, I returned back to the office for coffee and to warm-up. As I was drinking my coffee at my desk, I was eagerly awaiting people to call me on the phone to have me come out to list their homes for sale. Yes, I felt certain someone would call me that day! Sadly, it never happened. In fact, days two, three, four, and five went by with no one asking me to come out and provide the free market analysis. I must admit, I was a little discouraged. Growing a real estate career is a lot like planting seeds in a garden; you have to plant the seeds to reap the success. So I reminded myself that I had indeed planted seeds on that cold day. However, I needed to continue to fertilize and work my garden (farm area) to see future results.

One summer day, approximately six months later, I received a call. The caller asked if I could come out and talk to her about selling a piece of property. Yes, you guessed it; this home was located in my farm area. And after a few minutes at the home visiting with the homeowner (whom I had never met in person back on that cold, snowy day), she showed me a piece of paper they had found between their screen door and front door. There in her hand was a faded, wrinkled paper coupon with my name on it. She asked me if my offer was still valid. Of course I said yes.

Not only did I provide this lady with her free CMA, but I also listed her house and sold her property. She purchased another home from me, and then referred me to her mother, whose home I also listed and sold. Both this customer and her mother referred future business to me over many years. Farming a geographical area and prospecting for fifty to sixty minutes one morning, has provided thousands of dollars in commissions to my real estate business. I could share story after story like this one, where sending out postcards to a farm area, knocking on doors, and many other tried and true methods listed in this book have produced great results.

Many times agents will ask me how they can contact a farm area throughout the entire year. Actually, it's quite easy, especially when you set up a yearly plan. Here are some ideas to use for marketing in your farm area throughout the year, taken from my book *5-Minutes to Maximizing Technology*. Notice that each topic tends to go perfectly with the time of the year, making your monthly visit a meaningful one. Some of the suggestions listed in the table employ some of today's latest technology tools, such as podcasting (audio recordings that can consist of interviews with guests or other real estate related topics that are recorded and hosted on your website). Think of ways you can use YouTube, Twitter, and other new mediums to become the local expert, and drive traffic to your website for more information and details.

Month/Date	Topic	Detailed Description
January	**Taxes**	Interview a local CPA or tax advisor in your marketplace about tax preparation and organization of information to prepare annual income tax returns.
February	**Home Organization**	Consider interviewing someone from Lowe's or a local company that specializes in closet or home organization on how consumers can better organize their home closets, kitchen or other storage facilities.
March	**Gardening Tips**	Talk to a local nursery or area garden club president or member to get ideas and information about spring planting. By utilizing a local gardening club representative you will enable them to tell other garden club members about the podcasts which will in turn help drive people to your website to hear what their club member has to offer.
April	**Update on local housing market**	This is a good time for you to do a podcast and talk about what is going on in the local housing market, average sales price, days on the market and other information about the local housing area.
May	**Travel**	Interview a local travel representative or company about ideas for short and long vacations and where the best bargains tend to be for the upcoming travel season. As with other interviews of local people this is another great way to help promote your podcast website. Encourage the local travel agency to tell inquiries about the interview and how they can listen and get ideas on your website. In fact they may even promote your website in their advertisements and marketing materials.
June	**Summer camps and recreation**	Contact any local schools or community organizations that provide summer camps or recreational activities for kids during the summer.
July	**Local Government Update**	Consider interviewing someone from your local government such as the mayor, council member, an assessor or tax collector from your county government to provide information on what is happening at the local or county government level.
August	**School**	This is an excellent opportunity for you to interview the local school principal or other representative about registration, the school calendar or other activities and information students and parents should be aware of for the coming school year. Don't forget to prepare calendars or other types of marketing pieces such as a refrigerator magnet or postcard showing the days students will be out for holidays in the upcoming school year too! Encourage your listeners to call in, write or send an e-mail for their free copy. Note: By asking your listeners to send an e-mail for a calendar, you're able to capture new e-mail addresses and utilize permission-based marketing to hopefully communicate with these consumers on a regular basis through the Internet.

Month/Date	Topic	Detailed Description
September	Home Tips/Winterization	Consider talking to a local builder, contractor or someone from a building supply store to discuss ways and ideas consumers can make repairs to their home to save on utility costs. Winterization tips and other ideas would be excellent to include during this podcast as you interview your expert.
October	Housing Market Update	Since most consumers feel the winter is not a good time to sell property, this would be an excellent podcast to talk about just how good it is to continue to market property during the winter months. Although the market may be slow and consumers may not be as amped to purchase at the time the market is slower, it does provide for less competition for a home seller. You can also update consumers on what the market is doing at this time.
November	Cooking	Invite a local grocery store that may offer cooking classes, or someone who might offer kitchen parties to be a part of your November podcast to talk about Holiday menu and recipe ideas. As noted earlier this is an excellent way to promote your podcast since someone who offers home cooking parties and sells cooking accessories can in turn tell their guests about the podcast and give out information about your website. This will help provide more traffic to your website and podcast.
December	Home Safety Tips	Invite someone from the local fire department to help discuss tips consumers can incorporate around their home to provide safe conditions for the family.

Summary

Remember, working your farm may not produce immediate results. On the other hand, I have witnessed agents who went out, knocked on doors, and came back with a listing the same day. But don't look at farming as a "get rich quick" real estate method.

Farming a real estate area takes hard work: planting the seeds, fertilizing the soil, pulling the weeds, and tilling the ground consistently throughout the year. When you can develop and correctly work a specific, geographical farm area, the benefits can be amazing! And yes, it's just one of many ways you can jumpstart your real estate career!

The balance of the pages in this chapter provides you with some sample letters you might consider sending to your sphere of influence. If you have an interest in more letters like those featured, visit all of the 5-Minutes books for real estate agents at OnCourse Learning, Amazon, or my website, http://www.BusinessTechGuy.com.

[Date]

Address Block

Greeting Line

Hi, my name is *[Agent's Name]*, and I recently listed the real estate at *[listing address]* in your neighborhood. Do you know of some people you would like to have as neighbors? If so, please pass along my business card and a copy of the enclosed flyer to them. I can also arrange a preview of the property for your friends should they decide to look at this lovely home.

Thank you for your time, and if you're ever in the market to know the value of your property, call me for a FREE price evaluation on your house. I'll be glad to provide this information for you.

Sincerely,

[Agent Name]
[Agent Title]

From "5 Minutes to a Great Real Estate Letter" – OnCourse Learning

[Date]

Address Block

Greeting Line

Hello, my name is *[Agent's Name]*, with *[Agency Name]*. I am working with some buyers who expressed an interest in a home in your *[Area or Subdivision]*. Are you interested in selling your house? If so, I would be happy to visit with you to discuss what your house is worth on today's real estate market. Best of all, this consultation is FREE, and you are under no obligation to list or sell through me.

Now is a great time to buy or sell real estate!

I appreciate your time. Please call me if you have an interest in selling your house.

Yours truly,

[Agent Name]
[Agent Title]

From "5 Minutes to a Great Real Estate Letter" – OnCourse Learning

[Date]

Address Block

Greeting Line

Did you know all agents are not the same? That's right; not everyone offers the same services, or sells real estate in the same way. If you are in the market to buy or sell a home, let me show you how my real estate marketing system is different from that of the average real estate agent.

For a FREE price evaluation of what your property is worth in today's market, call me at *[your phone number]*. There are no high-pressure tactics and no obligation to list your house with me.

I appreciate your time and I hope to hear from you soon.

Sincerely,

[Agent Name]
[Agent Title]

From "5 Minutes to a Great Real Estate Letter" – OnCourse Learning

[Date]

Address Block

Greeting Line

Hello, my name is *[Agent's Name]*, and I am a real estate agent with *[Agency Name]*. I noticed that you own a house at *[address of property]* in *[City]*. Because the property is vacant, I wonder if you might consider selling it? Now is an excellent time to sell real estate, and many of our agents at *[Agency Name]* have potential buyers who cannot find the right home currently for sale through our local Multiple Listing Service.

If you consider selling this property, please allow me to do a FREE price evaluation for you. There's no pressure to list or sell through my company. I provide this service to many customers who want to know the value of their properties on today's real estate market. It also gives people an opportunity to meet me and learn more about my services, so when they are ready to sell they can make an informed decision.

You can visit my website at *[web address]* to learn more about me and view current listings for sale in your area. I appreciate your time, and again, feel free to call me if I can help in any way.

Sincerely,

[Agent Name]
[Agent Title]

From "5 Minutes to a Great Real Estate Letter" – OnCourse Learning

Chapter 13

Open Houses that Win Business

Open Houses

Most new real estate agents tend to gravitate toward working with buyers as their primary source of real estate leads. As noted in Chapter 10, your friends, family members, and coworkers can all provide you with possible leads for both buyers and sellers. However, if you want to begin seriously trying to work with potential buyers, holding open houses is a good starting point.

> "Working open houses is an excellent source for locating potential real estate leads."

Granted, as a new real estate licensee, you may not have many active properties listed for sale in which you can hold open. Don't let that discourage you. There are many real estate associates within your office who have properties they may like to have held as an open house. However, I must give a forewarning, some agents within your office may try to throw cold water on holding open houses. Yes, you will hear from many in your office that holding open houses is a waste of time. With that said, let me be one of the positive agents encouraging you to consider holding open houses, as I have sold several houses through this marketing activity, and I highly recommend it.

Many will try to discourage you from this marketing activity, or even provide negative feedback on why you should not hold open houses. However, open houses may provide visitors, who in turn may want to purchase a home. Yes, many of your visitors may be neighbors curious about what the home looks like. Others may be buyers who do not qualify to purchase (today), but the odds are in your favor that a certain percentage of your guests at your open house are folks who would love to own a home! It's your job to get their contact information, build a positive relationship, and help them find the right home. Understand that most of the time visitors at your open house may not particularly be interested in the property you are holding open, but as you discuss their needs and visit with them about their wants and desires, you normally will discover what exactly it is they are looking for. With that said, you have a new prospect, so get busy finding them a home that fits their needs!

As noted earlier, sometimes your guest to your open house may in fact be a neighbor within the subdivision or down the street. And yes, these open house visitors (neighbors) may also be considering placing their home for sale. Their visit to your open house may be a scouting mission to determine whether their home is worth more or less then the subject property being held open. And yes again, this could be an opportunity to obtain a new listing. Don't underestimate the power of holding an open house!

Open House Game Plan – Active vs. Passive

If you plan to hold houses open, you need to consider creating an active game plan. Most real estate agents I know go into an open house marketing program in a passive mode. In other words, there's not much work put into their marketing activity for holding an open house. Sadly, the real estate agent who tries to conduct a passive open house is missing out on a good opportunity.

When I suggest you create an active game plan, I am recommending the following:

- Send out pre-open house cards or letters to the neighborhood, announcing the date and time of your open house.

- Make sure you have a detailed brochure or flyer with one page about yourself and your company (see the chapter on creating a one-page resume).

- Prepare an open house registry, specifically where you can capture the name, address, phone number, and email address. Note, you should always complete the first line of your open house registry. This will help other arriving guests do the same.

- Map out in advance where you plan to put your open house pointer signs.

- Make certain you have contracts and other important documents and forms about this property available on-site.

- Possibly prepare a short printout from your MLS on other properties in this subdivision or ZIP Code.

- If you are not familiar with the property, preview the home in advance. If it is another agent's listing, have the listing agent or owners provide specific details about boundary markers, average utility costs, taxes, homeowner association dues etc.

- Plan to have the property advertised, if possible, in the local newspaper.

- Post property as open, with dates and times, in the MLS and your website and the company website.

- Be ready to post on social networking sites. A word of *caution to agents: you need to make certain the proper safety precautions are taken prior to holding any open house. Check with your owner and broker for more information, and if possible, always take someone with you to sit alongside at your open house.*

- Prepare a checklist for what you plan to do the day of the open house—before, during, and after.

- Be sure to send thank you cards to everyone who comes through the open house.

- Add any and all contacts who visited the open house into some type of a follow-up action plan.

- Send the listing agent a thank you card if this is not your listing.

- Send the sellers a thank you card for allowing you to hold their home open.

As you can easily determine from the list above, actively engaging in your open house marketing efforts takes some work. I emphasize having some type of checklist or action plan for your open house.

Open House Checklist	
Open House To Do's	**Completed**
Schedule a convenient date for open house with clients	
Arrange to have open house date and time posted on MLS	
Arrange to have open house date posted to company and personal websites	
Arrange to have open house date and time posted to other Internet web portals	
Write a blog post or prepare a YouTube video about your upcoming open house to place on your website	
Send postcards to surrounding neighbors announcing your open house, date and time	
Walk the neighborhood and knock on doors announcing your upcoming open house	
Provide sellers with instructions for staging home and securing valuables	
Prepare flyers for open house, including comparable homes you have for sale	
Arrange for lender pre-qualification forms and financing examples for potential buyers	
Secure the appropriate number of open house signs and pointer arrows needed	
Research any and all sign ordinances and map out where potential open house pointer and directional signs may be placed	
Have balloons for open house signs	
Prepare a guest registry form for attendees to sign	

Open House Checklist	
Open House To Do's	Completed
Include a sample sales contract to have at open house	
At conclusion of open house, send thank-you card to sellers	
Prepare a detailed report on property from your Multiple Listing Service or through another CMA program showing the property value compared to other recently sold homes in the area	
Research competitive properties in the same area, have copies of information for those properties available if questions arise	
Prepare a PowerPoint® slide show of other homes for sale and/or your services to display on your laptop or tablet device while visitors tour your open house	
Make sure you have plenty of water, light snacks, chair, and a notepad	
Obtain any office literature or printouts you may provide consumers about you, your firm, or about buying and selling real estate	
Send thank-you notes to all attendees	
Send thank-you notes to anyone who allowed you to place an open house sign or arrow on their property	
Put guests on active follow-up plan	
Begin planning and scheduling your next open house	

You may think of additional items to include with your open house checklist, but hopefully this will give you a good start. Remember that having an active open house program will enable you to capture the right information and reach the maximum number of potential prospects for this property.

As important as introducing yourself as a real estate agent is to the public, you also have to remember to always play it safe as well. Safety is a big concern for every real estate agent. When you hold an open house, remember these safety tips:

Open House Safety Tips

- Avoid holding open houses alone

- Make sure you have a mobile phone

- Determine all possible escape routes

- Park in front of home, NOT the driveway
- Leave your business card with date and time of arrival
- Keep the door locked until someone arrives
- Keep a notebook to make notes
- Stay near an exit when showing a property
- Avoid walking in front of prospects
- Check in with office or family often
- Have owners tell the neighbors about your open house

Finally, as noted before, do not underestimate the power of holding an open house. Think of your open house as a form of prospecting. By visiting neighbors in the area, announcing your open house, sending out cards, and of course, meeting possible visitors, you can generate future prospects to help jumpstart your real estate business! Just remember to always play it safe!

> **"Think of your open house as a form of prospecting."**

The remaining pages in this chapter provide you with some sample letters you might consider using to send to your sphere of influence. If you have an interest in more letters like those featured, visit all of the "5 Minutes" books for real estate agents at OnCourse Learning, Amazon, or my website, http://www.BusinessTechGuy.com.

[Date]

Address Block

Greeting Line

I am holding an open house this weekend in your neighborhood at *[address of property]*. If you know someone who might have an interest in this home, please let that person know about my open house. Viewing will take place on *[day of open house]* from *[time of open house]*.

Are you interested in selling your house, or would you like to know what its value is on today's real estate market? For a free price evaluation, call me at *[your phone number]*. There are no high-pressure tactics, and there is no obligation to list your house. Best of all, it's FREE!

I appreciate your time, and don't forget my open house this *[day of open house]* from *[time of open house]*.

Sincerely,

[Agent Name]
[Agent Title]

From "5 Minutes to a Great Real Estate Letter" – OnCourse Learning

[Date]

Address Block

Greeting Line

I wanted to say *thank you* for taking time out of your busy schedule to visit my open house this past weekend at *[address of open house]*. I hope you enjoyed the tour and hope the additional information about the house was sufficient for you. If you would like to view more information about this home, please check out my website at *[your web address]*.

Would you like to be the first to learn of new listings in your area? If so, please call or write me at *[your phone number and e-mail address]* and provide me with a brief description of what you are looking for. I can set up a saved search in our Multiple Listing Service to notify both you and me of new listings the instant they're placed on the market. There's no cost or obligation for me to do this for you, and, best of all, we'll both have firsthand knowledge of those great buys that become available before anyone else.

Again, *[Letter Name]*, *thank you* for visiting my open house, and please let me know if I can help you in any way with your real estate needs.

Yours truly,

[Agent Name]
[Agent Title]

From "5 Minutes to a Great Real Estate Letter" – OnCourse Learning

Chapter 14

Direct Mail –
Today's Hidden Marketing Gem

Direct Mail

A large portion of my real estate career has focused on direct mailings. Direct mailings are easy and efficient ways to communicate with your sphere of influence and other contacts within your database. Direct mail is also a good return on your investment, despite what others may claim. According to Target Marketing Magazine, direct mail beats social media advertising for return on investment for both businesses to consumers marketing, as well as business-to-business. Direct mail also boasted a higher response rate than social media advertising and response rates, which can reach as high as 6.5 percent. Note the average response rate according to Target Marketing Magazine is approximately two percent.

I also believe direct mail is aligned for bigger numbers in the future. In today's electronic age, with texting, email and other forms of communication, letters and correspondence are once again actually enjoyable to receive. It's not uncommon for me to go to my mailbox and find one or two pieces of mail to open. Most of my bills today are paperless and arrive via email. Many of my friends and business associates communicate to me by text or email. And what few pieces of U.S. postal mail I receive is no fun. Let's face it; it's nice to receive a personal note or card from a friend when you open your mailbox!

I believe people enjoy receiving a letter or a card from time to time, especially if the correspondence is done so that it attracts your attention and is appealing to you.

If you do plan to offer direct mailings to your farm area, sphere of influence, or any other type of marketing endeavor, I would encourage you to think about when and how you send out your direct mail pieces. The United States Post Office has a wealth of information on its website to assist with direct mailings. Visit https://www.usps.com/business/advertise-with-mail.htm for more information.

Most people who use direct mail marketing will use bland type fonts for their envelopes, and even go as far as to use bulk mailing permits stamped on their envelopes. Most consumers who recognize mailing pieces as being termed junk mail will normally throw them away or tear them up without even opening the envelope. This is why I believe it is so important for you to think about how your envelope and information is displayed to the consumer, and to always send your mailings first class.

> **"It is so important for you to think about how your envelope and information displays to the consumer."**

My good friend and real estate training coach Corky Hyatt taught me a valuable lesson many years ago in my Graduate REALTOR® Institute marketing course. During this class, Corky had all of the students in the room close their eyes for a brief moment. Corky then asked us to imagine that we were walking out to our mailboxes. "As you open the mailbox, Corky instructed, "reach inside and grab the various pieces of information, and begin casually scanning the pieces of mail you've received". Corky then asked, *"Which piece of mail would you open first?"* Immediately my answer was the piece of mail that is personally addressed to me. Yes, it is probably in a different colored card or envelope format. If it looks as though it is from a friend or has some type of mysterious intrigue about it, I would definitely be interested. Keep this in mind when using direct mail marketing.

Make certain when you address the names in your database that you use a type of font that is perhaps a handwritten signature font, or use something else that would be appealing. If possible, try to use different types of envelopes or colors and sizes. Sometimes you can go to a card store or perhaps a retailer who sells cards and ask them if they have any envelopes left over you can have or purchase. You might even go to your local office supply store to request extra envelopes they may have. Look online and purchase envelopes that are made in different colors and sizes. Make sure your mailings do not give off the standard impression as being junk mail.

The point for this exercise is to remind you that direct mail marketing needs to be different and look personal. Many of the chapters in this book discuss ways of corresponding with various databases and groups of individuals. I encourage you to create interesting and clever marketing pieces that will gain the attention of your contacts. Yes, you will be communicating with many of these groups through the U.S. Postal Service. To make certain that your mail and marketing pieces are delivered and opened is an important part of your direct mail marketing campaign. I encourage you to take the time to study various ways and strategies, and discover how direct mail marketing can benefit your real estate career.

I have included several types of correspondence and examples of direct mail marketing for your consideration on the following pages.

140 Chapter 14

Figure 14-1 Postcard Example with Price Evaluation Coupon - Courtesy of John Mayfield, Mayfield Real Estate Inc.

Figure 14-2 Postcard Example with Featured Homes - Courtesy of John Mayfield, Mayfield Real Estate Inc.

New Office Location:

304 N. Washington St.—Farmington, MO 63640

Same Great Service, 573-756-0077

Offer Not Intended to solicit business if you are currently under a contract with another agency.

John D. Mayfield, CRB, e-PRO, GRI
Real Estate Broker/Author/Speaker
JohnM@MayfieldRE.com — www.MayfieldRE.com
Helping Thousands of Families with their real estate needs since 1978

1st 4 Months 20115

Thinking about buying or selling real estate? Call John today, "Experience Counts!"

City	Average Sales Price	Days on Market	Number Closed	Price Per Sq. Ft.
Farmington	$126,725	89	57	$74
Park Hills	$46,871	80	26	$36
Desloge	$68,065	71	13	$54
Bonne Terre	$68,646	83	24	$50

Information based on Sales from January 1st, 2015 through April 30th, 2011 The data was compiled on May 25th, 2015 @ 4:00 p.m. +/-, and is subject to change if information is added or deleted after this date/time. Mineral Area MLS, Single-Family Residential Sales Only.

Figure 14-3 Postcard Example Showing Sales Experience - Courtesy of John Mayfield, Mayfield Real Estate Inc.

Chapter 15

Online Marketing Strategies for
Your Real Estate Business

Creating an Online Marketing Strategy

My friend and New York Times best-selling author Jay Baer discusses the importance of helping consumers solve problems as the next big online marketing strategy. Jay's book, *Youtility: Why Smart Marketing Is about Help, Not Hype*, provides some fascinating statistics and facts about small businesses that are winning the online war through helping consumers solve problems and much more.

Creating a "Youtility" marketing strategy is about helping consumers understand how to use your products and services. For example, one story Jay Baer shares in his book is about a swimming pool business in Virginia. At the height of the economic downturn, River Pools and Spas was close to going out of business. Let's face it; people really don't want to purchase a swimming pool during an economic downturn when the majority of their focus is on surviving financially and making certain their mortgage payment is made each and every month. But Marcus Sheridan, co-owner of River Pools and Spas, decided to create a blog, and through his blog began writing helpful articles consumers could use about swimming pool ownership. It was similar to frequently asked questions, and the blog answered many questions swimming pool owners (or those wanting to be owners) might have about this luxury homeownership item. Despite the gloom and doom during this economic downturn, Marcus Sheridan decided to begin blogging as a marketing strategy. As Jay points out in his book, Sheridan turned his business around and became one of the biggest swimming pool businesses in his area.[1]

What can we learn from River Pools and Spas and this type of helpful blogging marketing strategy? First, we can apply the same principles, as real estate professionals, to our businesses. Real estate is one of the most complex purchasing decisions consumers face, and most people have no idea what they are doing or how to purchase a home.

Here's where your expertise and all of that great information you learned in pre-license real estate school can be useful. Consider using videos, audios, and blogs to guide the consumer through this complicated and sometimes scary real estate jungle.

Thought you would never use the income valuation while studying appraisals in the real world? Now you can explain what "uncle IRV" (income divided by rate equals value) means, ensuring that consumers know what the advantages and disadvantages with this income appraisal method for investment-producing properties means.

Yes, I'm sure you never thought you would discuss the habendum clause (otherwise known as the "to have and to hold clause," which gives the new owner the legal right to absolute ownership) once you finished your pre-license real estate classes and exam. Now it becomes a tool you can

---

[1] *Youtility: Why Smart Marketing Is about Help Not Hype*. 1st ed. Vol. 1. New York: Penguin Group, 2013. Print.

use to explain how this real estate terminology is applicable to the consumer, through a short video snippet on your real estate blog post. Hopefully, you can begin to see the advantages of what you've learned, and how you can share this information with others in your marketplace.

Here's the beauty of using the Internet, YouTube, and various social media platforms, as a real estate professional: You can strengthen your SEO (Search Engine Optimization) for your website so that people who are searching for information or keywords in search engines such as Google will be pulled into your website, optimizing your viewing potential as you post this type of information. When someone is searching for a good or service, or perhaps the meaning of a valuation model for real estate investment property, you just might pop up in the search results. If the consumer clicks on the link and lands on your website, they may find more information at your website and identify you as the expert. They may even dial your phone number or send you an email inquiring about the possibility of doing business with you!

You may laugh at that scenario and think this is a far-fetched example of earning business, but this is exactly what Jay Baer explains in his book. Consumers are using the Internet and our wired world to find help and more information about the goods and services they plan to use.[2] By posting information online, you're positioning yourself as a savvy expert in the field. Just make sure you're not giving advice as a legal, tax, or finance expert (unless you're licensed to do so).

Have you ever gone to search for something on Google, Bing®, or Yahoo!®, found the results, and ended up taking action through that particular website that provided your answer? Most people would answer yes, and even more people will continue to do this in the future as generations who never knew life without the Internet come of age and start doing business.

Although Internet marketing may not jumpstart your real estate career as quickly as utilizing your sphere of influence database or prospecting expired or for-sale-by-owners would, it should be a part of your marketing strategy and your business plan for growing your real estate profession. After all, more and more consumers are turning to the Internet to look for real estate and to find answers to their real estate questions. In fact, according to the most recent study by the National Association of REALTORS® Profile of Homebuyers and Sellers (2014), ninety percent of buyers used the Internet during the home buying process to search for properties for sale.

> **"More and more consumers are turning to the Internet to look for real estate and to find answers to their real estate questions."**

As with any marketing strategy discussed in this book, consistency, patience, and hard work are all required to reap the fruits and benefits of your labors. Utilizing the Internet as a tool

---

[2]*Youtility: Why Smart Marketing Is about Help Not Hype.* 1st ed. Vol. 1. New York: Penguin Group, 2013. Print.

in your marketing plan is no exception to this rule. Unfortunately, there are no get-rich-quick schemes when it comes to building a real estate brand. You have to be doing a little bit of everything discussed in the book to see the fruits of your labor come to fruition.

What are some other online marketing strategies you might consider when using Jay Baer's utility method for creation of content? YouTube videos are excellent media strategies to consider for delivering your message. More consumers are utilizing YouTube today as one of their search engine choices. YouTube, at one time, was the second most used site as a search engine when consumers needed to look for answers to questions they have. There is an endless amount of topics that can be done to help drive Internet users to your YouTube channel while providing informative clips about purchasing, selling, or maintaining homes. A short video about how to obtain a VA (Veterans Administration) loan or first-time homebuyer financing are good examples for buyers. Shooting a video with a home inspector or an interior designer or home stager might be interesting and beneficial for buyers. Videos might also be developed to describe some of the various real estate terminologies or to explain title insurance, along with the different types of deeds used. It is important to remember, however, that these videos do not have to be professionally done. The predominant amount of videos that are viewed on Youtube are not professionally produced. This real-life look typically draws in viewers in much larger numbers than the professionally done videos. However, that being said, you want your videos to be shot with as steady a hand (ideally using a tripod or steadying stick) as possible, with clean audio that can be heard with ease. Very simplistic editing (such as starting and stopping your footage at a certain point, as well as minimizing shaking) can be done directly through YouTube. There are also a few software programs like Vimeo, iMovie®, and Wondershare™ that can be used to do more effective tweaking of your videos.

Some consumers are not visual learners and perhaps do not want to watch videos. In fact, some customers have slow Internet connections, making video hard to stream from a computer or a mobile phone.

Many consumers may be using a smartphone or a tablet as their only Internet-connected device, and they may prefer to read an article rather than watch a video. In those situations, consider writing a blog to meet the needs of those consumers. Blogs can range from how to prepare your home for sale, statistics about the local marketplace, and financing topics, to other new trends and marketing suggestions to help sell real estate quickly and for top dollar. When a buyer or seller asks you a question, make a mental note and write the question down. Chances are it will make an excellent blog post to consider for your website.

Younger consumers may be interested in listening to a podcast. Your job as a real estate professional is to be conscious of providing information to all potential consumers in various formats. For example, I produced a two-minute tech tip revolving around technology, showing real estate agents how technology can be used to make more sales and be more productive. I make my tech tips available on my website at www.businesstechguy.com so that once a consumer is on the site after possibly having searched for certain information outlined in my podcast, they will have access to my other information and marketing material as well.

I've recently begun stripping the audio off of the two-minute tech tips and posting them as podcasts. The podcasts (audio only) are pushed out to iTunes®, a popular site consumers use to download audios to their iPhones® and computers. I then use a program called Dragon® dictation to transcribe the audio. Once the audio has been transcribed, I can go into my word processor and begin editing the document. I can now post this information as a written blog article on my website. Some marketers call this re-purposing content. Although I have used an example from technology business for repurposing short concentrated content to consumers, you can use the same concept for real estate consumers in your marketplace. Consider providing a two-minute market update for your area, or a weekly video showcase of new listings that have come on the market.

Hopefully, you can see how I have taken the video, repurposed it as an audio-only podcast, and then formatted it into a written blog post. If a consumer wants to watch the video, it's there. Should they desire to listen to this information as an audio podcast while driving in their car, it's available. What about the consumer who says, "I hate audio, and I despise watching videos; please let me read something on your website"? Great news, they are in luck, because it's available for them as well!

As a real estate professional, you need to be conscious of how you can re-purpose your content. How can you begin providing your information in various formats on your website? E-books are very popular, and today many short books and informational topics can be easily converted into e-book formats for consumers to download to the specific device they use. We'll talk more about opt-in marketing in just a moment, because that's a large part of your online marketing strategy. But understanding the importance of re-purposing and creating content that can be available in a wide variety of formats is important for you to consider. Remember, not everyone likes chocolate ice cream. You need to have other choices available in order to win all consumers who may come into contact with you and your website.

Create an Opt-In Piece

Here's what you need to know about your website. First of all, most people don't spend much time on your website! I hate to burst your bubble, and I realize some of you are spending a lot of money each month to have a customized website, but facts are facts, and the majority of people spend very little time looking around most websites.

Second, most websites are like empty offices. That's right, visitors come to your website at all hours of the day and night, and guess what? Nobody's there! Your website is like one big empty office, with no one available for the consumer to talk with at the exact moment the consumer wants. Yes, perhaps while you are reading this section, a cash buyer just visited your personal or company website, looked around, and left, never leaving their name, phone number or email address for future contact.

If both situations described above are true, how can you stop the leakages and loss of leads, and begin to capture the names and contact information of people who visit your online office? It's easy; create what is called an "opt-in" piece! Provide consumers with the opportunity to sign up for a free offer or something of value you are giving away from your website.

> "Provide consumers with the opportunity to sign up for a free offer or something of value you are giving away from your website."

For example, what about a FREE e-book on *How to Save Thousands on Your Next Home Purchase?* A sample copy of this is available as a supplemental resource to this book.

Figure 15-1   Offering a Free E-book as an Enticement to Customers - Courtesy of John Mayfield, Mayfield Real Estate Inc.

I transferred the information to the Apple Keynote slide presentation program, added a few graphics, and then saved it as a PDF file. (One of my favorite resources for graphics, audios and a wide variety of resources to use for creating content is www.market.envato.com.) I can now create a customized landing page or link, and offer this free e-book to consumers who visit my website. Once they provide me with their name and e-mail address, the free e-book is delivered to them automatically, regardless of the time of day, or where I might be located.

Now that I have the consumer's name and e-mail address, it is my obligation to stay in touch with the potential client, and cultivate and nurture the relationship until a sale on real estate can be consummated.

By creating an opt-in piece, you now increase the odds of capturing those missed opportunities (leads) that visit your website. The key is to provide an attractive, eye-appealing offer that the consumers want.

My *5 Minutes to Great Real Estate Marketing Ideas* book has several excellent reports, letters, postcard examples, and other marketing designs for helping you grow your real estate business. Many of the solutions in the book make excellent examples and marketing pieces for creating free offers you can provide through your website. For example, buyers may have an interest in knowing about purchasing a home: *"Avoiding the Ten Biggest Pitfalls when Buying a Home,"* or *"How to Save Thousands on Your Next Home Purchase."* Everything from how to stage your home for generating the maximum purchase price, to effective strategies to consider when purchasing a home are all effective ideas you might consider. Leverage these types of examples to create short informative e-books that will invite interest and create a good call to action for consumers to opt-in, allowing you to create and develop a business relationship.

Summary

This chapter discusses ways you can use your website and other online tools to help consumers understand the buying and selling process. Think about the various ways one piece of your content can be delivered to the market. Discover strategies and opt-in pieces to capture consumers' contact information when they visit your website. What follows are some reports from my book *5 Minutes to Great Real Estate Marketing Ideas* that I believe make excellent free opt-in pieces you might consider using.

And finally, stay in touch, and build a relationship by communicating with your new leads regularly. When you can follow and implement this simple online marketing plan, you will be well on your way to jumpstarting your real estate career!

Avoiding the Ten Biggest Pitfalls when Buying a Home

1. Failing to have your real estate agent provide detailed market analysis on your home's value.

2. Failing to get a building inspection on the residence you are purchasing.

3. Neglecting to have a full staked survey on the property you are purchasing.

4. Making a low-ball offer and discouraging the seller from negotiating with you.

5. Failing to get prequalified for a loan prior to making the offer to purchase.

6. Not allowing enough time to complete all of the necessary building and title examinations and inspections.

7. Neglecting to work with buyer's agent.

8. Purchasing a FSBO or other real estate without the use of a real estate professional or attorney.

9. Purchasing a parcel of real estate without obtaining title insurance.

10. Not obtaining a city inspection!

Although the items listed here are not a full and comprehensive list of pitfalls or mistakes buyers can make when purchasing a home, they are issues that come up from time to time and tend to be problem areas for many buyers. You can avoid having such situations by using the right real estate agent. That's why *[agent's name]* is available and ready to serve you. For a more comprehensive explanation about some of the issues listed in this report, call *[agent's name]* at *[phone number]* so that I can be more thorough in explaining how these areas can be a possible determent to your next home purchase. I would also love to visit with you and put you on my computerized real estate listing. Search through our Multiple Listing Service so that you can be the first to find out about new listings that become available. For more information. Visit my website at *[web address]* or email me at *[email address]*.

Why Every Buyer Should Get a Home Inspection

This is not a comprehensive list of needs for a home inspection, nor should this report be relied on solely for the purchase of your next home. It is just a guide that can help you understand the benefits of having a home inspection prior to your next real estate purchase.

- Most sales contracts provide for the buyer to perform various inspections on the property within so many days after signing the sales contract. By having a qualified and recommended home inspector look at the property under consideration, you have the opportunity to find any major or structural defects in advance of the home purchase. This inspection and notification of the issues at hand can allow you, the borrower, to either cancel or void the contract, or request the seller to make the necessary repairs prior to signing any closing documents. Of course, state laws and the contract verbiage will dictate the final outcome, but it is important to make sure the party representing you in the transaction includes the opportunity to have a building inspection of the property you plan to purchase.

- The inspector will look for things you never dreamed of! Most building inspectors will look for a wide variety of items, both structurally and mechanically, that will be visible to you and me, as well as items that will not be visible during the normal inspection.

- The building inspector will provide you with a detailed report outlining the issues and problems that need to be corrected. It is important to use this detailed report when requesting corrections to the contract, or in the case of major structural defects, as it allows you the opportunity to terminate the contract. Of course, you will need to seek legal counsel on the verbiage in the contract before you can move forward on your decision. But a detailed report will normally be necessary to provide to the seller or seller's agent should this situation arise.

- Don't panic about everything. Remember, the building inspector's job is to find problems and issues with the sales contract. It is not critical that every detail pointed out in the contract be correct or repaired. Some minor issues listed in the inspection report may only take a half a day's work and a couple hundred dollars to correct.

- Although you should consult with your agent regarding the legalities of your detailed inspection report, don't feel that every listed item in the inspection is a cause for panic.

- Ask for recommendations. Prior to hiring a building inspector, it is always a good idea to ask for recommendations and find out what the satisfaction level has been with the inspector's past clients. You can not only request recommendations from building inspectors themselves, but you can also ask the real estate agent you are working with to provide a list of buyers who may have used one particular inspector or another. By doing this, you're sure to find out the positive or negative reactions of those who have worked with a given building inspector.

- Ask to see if the inspector is a member of any national organization. Some groups, such as the American Society of Home Inspectors (ASHI), require the inspector to meet certain criteria and to have a certain educational background to be certified as one of their inspectors. This rigorous requirement assures you that the inspector you are hiring meets all of the qualification criteria and the code for performing a home inspection for you. It also assures you that inspectors are recertifying themselves on a continuous and regular basis so that they are constantly updated and familiar with the current building codes and construction requirements.

- A home inspection is not all that you will need. Although most home inspectors do a good job finding areas in need of repair and problem issues with the home you are planning to purchase, some cities and government municipalities require a separate occupancy inspection and permit prior to your moving into your future residence.

Just because the building inspector investigates your home and finds little or no problem areas, occasionally the city inspector may have a newly updated list and will require certain changes to be made to the home. Although most building inspectors will try to stay on top of these local city changes, occasionally one issue or area may fall through the cracks. It is a good idea to not only hire a building inspector but also to sign the necessary forms and documents and pay any local municipality fees so that the occupancy inspector can preview the home also.

- Don't forget local utility inspections. As noted in the previous bullet point for obtaining any local municipality occupancy inspections, it is also a good idea to have the local utility companies inspect the home for their required standards for turning on the utilities. Again, most inspectors do a good job looking at the utility requirements necessary during their home inspection, but occasionally the local gas company or electric company could have a requirement the building inspector is not aware of. It is always a good idea to cover all of your bases prior to closing so that an issue or problem does not arise after the seller has received the money and the contract dates have elapsed.

- Ask building inspectors what areas they do not cover and what additional inspections you might need. For example, some building inspectors are qualified to inspect for termites while others may not be. It is a good idea to make sure you know in advance what areas the inspector will not guarantee under his or her inspection.

- Order your inspection in advance. Remember, the sales contract will have important dates for you to follow to request changes to the home that are in the sales contract.

Please seek advice from your legal counsel or qualified real estate professional regarding these dates. But understand that waiting until the last minute can be detrimental and could possibly cost you thousands of dollars if an issue or problem needs to be corrected and your inspection period has expired.

All the above bullet points do not form a complete list of items that could arise regarding building inspections, but they are a good guide for you to use and remember prior to purchasing your next home. At *[agency name]* we would love to help you with your next home purchase. I have additional *free* reports listed on my website at *[web address]*, and you can also call me at *[agent's phone number]* for more information. I hope this report has been helpful for you, and I look forward to hearing from you soon. *[agent's name]*.

Chapter 16

Why **Accountability Matters**

Accountability

There are many pieces to the puzzle for becoming a successful real estate professional. As I have discussed throughout the book, business planning, marketing (both off-line and online), daily prospecting, and of course building a valuable database of friends, family members, coworkers, past customers, and clients are all critical to your success as a real estate agent. In fact, if you're serious about jumpstarting your real estate career (new or existing real estate professionals) it will require an overall implementation of the suggestions and recommendations in this book. You will also need to continue to learn and to gather additional ideas and strategies from your broker, coach and sales associates in your office.

To make certain that your real estate career remains on track and focused, you need to aim at a specific target. Having someone who can assist you with keeping a steady aim at your target (an accountability partner) is the final piece of the puzzle. After all, each of us can write down goals, envision a successful career in real estate, and tell others of our glorious plans for our real estate career. Yet if you do not keep yourself accountable to your goals and action plans, you may never end up hitting the target. Here is the $64,000 question: How does one hold himself or herself accountable? Believe it or not, there are several solutions to this question. This chapter will show you some ideas and possible ways to stay accountable to your goals and objectives.

Ways to Stay Accountable

Probably the most effective way to keep yourself accountable is by having a mentor or leader in your office. This should be someone you can confide in about your weekly activities. This person needs to be someone with whom you feel comfortable sharing your accomplishments and your defeats. You should find someone who is successful. Try to find a person who leads the office and will also speak honestly to you about suggestions and needed improvements to your career.

> **"You need someone who can keep you in check and provide the needed changes to keep you on track toward your goals."**

Let's think about this for just a moment. If you were trying to coach yourself, how difficult or challenging would you make the routine? Being your own coach will not work. If you do not have someone you can go to for help with staying accountable to your goals and plans, then who is keeping score? Hopefully, your office provides some sort of mentoring. If not, is there someone in your market with whom you've made a connection who can fill that role?

Your mentor or coach should be someone who understands where you want to go with your real estate career. They should also have the ability to suggest new ideas and strategies you may want to implement. Keep in mind, this is not something you have to do daily (although it would be helpful to have a daily team meeting). Your accountability partner needs to be someone you can visit with weekly. Most brokers and managers, especially leaders in a larger office, may not have the luxury of meeting with you weekly. Again, this will depend on the size and number of agents your organization has on its roster, as well as the duties and assignments your manager may incur. Still, it is important for you to remain in close contact for a few moments or longer with your accountability partner. At a bare minimum you should meet with your accountability partner to go over your goals, plans, and activities from the past week.

Keep Your Goals and Actions in Writing

I remember in my personal fitness life that I was required to write down the exercise performed, how many repetitions I performed, and the amount of weight and the number of times this exercise was executed. I kept my progress by recording this information into a notebook. Because of this record keeping, I was able to track my achievements and watch my improvement over a period of time. It also helped me understand where my weaknesses were. For example, if I took a few days off and did not lift weights the number of repetitions I performed would be lower than what I had done during my previous session. In fact, oftentimes I had to lower the amount of weight to successfully perform the exercises. It was an excellent reminder of the fact that if I took too much time off from exercising and lifting weights, my productivity would actually diminish. The same principle is true for your real estate career and tracking your results. If you are not doing a lot of the things you have set out to do, the results will probably show up during your conversations and feedback with your mentor.

With that said, keep a journal! This may seem a little challenging and difficult, but if you want to jumpstart your real estate career, you and your accountability partner need to know what you are doing right, and what you're doing wrong. Clearly, the only way that you can completely figure this out is through journaling your daily activities.

Take the time to jot down notes about what you do throughout each hour of the day. You might find this a little time-consuming; however, I am not suggesting you detail a complete essay or a minute-by-minute summary of your daily activities. The ideal implementation of this is to write a brief synopsis of what you did from nine to ten in the morning. For example, noting that you "called six for-sale-by-owners from nine to ten and followed-up with two current prospects" is sufficient for your activities. Of course, the more detailed the better, but don't go overboard spending too much time on this activity.

You need to be honest about your activities and what you are doing with your time throughout your business day. You should then take your daily totals and summarize the information into a weekly recap. This information will be helpful when sharing with your coach what transpired throughout the week. In fact, you might even try to break the activities down by percentages for the week. Example, you spent twenty percent of the week prospecting during business hours, ten percent on social media, forty percent showing property, etc. Keeping good detailed notes about your activities for the week will again encourage you to know what you're doing with your time, as well as remind you of where you may need to improve. If you find yourself journaling that you checked your email, spent time on Facebook, read the news, etc., you will need to make some changes in your daily routine. Plus, you will have to share these sad results with your accountability partner.

A good mentor and coach who works to keep you accountable will set weekly goals and challenges for you. Most agents find this helpful, as they strive to make their weekly meetings productive and positive. Confessing to your coach that you completed your goals will give you a sense of accomplishment, not to mention the good it will do for your real estate business.

I have a goal right now to lose a certain amount of weight by March 1 of this year. My goal says I will weigh "X" or less by March 1st. By reading this goal each day when I wake up and before I go to bed (as well as various times throughout the day), I can stay on target and focused toward my goal. Each time I sit down to eat or think about a snack, I am reminded to make a positive choice that will help me reach my goal. The same principle will apply when journaling your daily activities and sharing them with your accountability partner. Even if you have to write down choices you made that were not beneficial to your short-term and long-term goals, you will continue to remind yourself of what you need to do to stay you on target.

Be Honest and Open

It is also important for you to be honest and straightforward with your accountability partner. If you did not make contacts or calls the previous week, or you failed to send out letters and your prospecting activities were zero, then tell it like it is. There is no need (nor will it be helpful) to be dishonest or try to sugarcoat your performance from the previous week for your coach or mentor. After all, how can your coach help you if you are not being honest about your previous week's activities?

Finally, don't panic if you miss a week with your coach, or if there is a period of time when you cannot visit with your accountability partner. Schedules can get hectic, and people may not be able to meet as regularly as intended. If you cannot meet because of a conflict or a problem, I suggest using an email program or a video email program like BombBomb™ or Eyejot™ to send a video email to your mentor, recapping what you have done throughout the week. If your mentor has the same program, perhaps he or she can reply to your email. With today's technology, there's really no reason why a person cannot keep in touch via Skype, video conferencing, or another online solution for coaching and mentoring. And if all else fails, a quick phone conversation will also work.

Summary

All of us have goals and visions for our real estate careers. You may know where you want to be in the future. You may have even written your goals down to look at daily. Perhaps you have a wide variety of marketing ideas and solutions on how you may find buyers or sellers to work with. And yes, you may even have some of the best checklists and action plans available. However, none of this may work if you do not have anyone to help keep you accountable on your daily goals and objectives. You need someone who can advise you on what you may be doing wrong, let you know what needs to be implemented, and provide a list of activities to do for the coming week. With that information in hand, you need to decide whether you will execute those solutions. Taking the information suggested by your mentor and using it is what will determine whether you will be successful as a real estate professional. Without accountability, you are fighting a fight that you cannot win. If you do not have someone who can help keep you accountable, how can you succeed?

If you truly want to jumpstart your real estate career, you need an accountability partner who will encourage, motivate, and suggest to you ways and ideas to help you stay on track.

Agent Weekly Accountability Scorecard

Activities Check each day activity is worked on. If activity is completed and your goal met, place an "X" in the appropriate win column. If not, place an "X" in the Loss column. Total up each section below, and then transfer totals to your year to date standings.	Sunday	Monday	Tuesday	Wednesday	Thursday	Friday	Saturday	Win	Loss
Prospecting Goals									
Made _____ phone calls to my sphere of influence (S.O.I.) list for the week.									
Contacted _____ for-sale-by-owner (fsbo) for the week									
Sent _____ expired listing letters for the week									
Made _____ follow-up calls or letters to fsbo or expired group for the week									
Mailed _____ post cards or letters to my S.O.I. for the week									
Made _____ personal visit to S.O.I. for the week									
Mailed a minimum of _____ thank you cards, or news related articles from paper for the week									
Totals									
Education and Personal Development									
Read _____ motivational article for the week									
Read a minimum of _____ days on a business or motivational /self-help book for the week									
Listened to a minimum of _____ minutes to a motivational, business or self-help tape/CD/MP3 for the week									
Spent a minimum of 10 minutes each day reciting positive affirmations about myself and my real estate career									
Read my "written" goals each day									
Planned my day the night before a minimum of _____ days									
Reviewed pending and active documents _____ times this week for missing information.									
Totals									

Copyright – © 2015 – John D. Mayfield, www.RealEstateSalesMeetings.com and www.RealEstateTechGuy.com

Figure 16-1 Accountability Scorecard - Courtesy of John Mayfield, Mayfield Real Estate Inc.

Activities Check each day activity is worked on. If activity is completed and your goal met, place an "X" in the appropriate win column. If not, place an "X" in the Loss column. Total up each section below, and then transfer totals to your year to date standings.	Sunday	Monday	Tuesday	Wednesday	Thursday	Friday	Saturday	Win	Loss
Quality Time and Community Service									
Encouraged or helped someone in my office this _____.									
Spent quality time with my family or loved ones this week.									
Spent time meditating, praying or reflecting on life _____ days this week.									
Spent time doing one activity I enjoy and am passionate about this week.									
Spent time doing one activity my loved one enjoys and is passionate about this week.									
Helped with one service activity for your church, community, or service organization you belong to this _____.									
Contributed financially to my church, community or other service organization this _____.									
Totals									
Health									
Exercised a minimum of _____ days									
Used healthy choices and decisions about what foods to eat _____ days this week.									
Practiced Yoga or Stretching _____ days this week. Time limit is optional.									
Flossed my teeth _____ days this week.									
Wore my seat belt _____% of the time I drove my automobile this week.									
Avoided excessive eating and drinking every day this week.									
Avoided one bad food or beverage item I like _____ days this week.									
Totals									

Scorecard Results	Year to Date		Last Week's Score Year to Date		This Week's Score	
	Wins	**Losses**	**Wins**	**Losses**	**Wins**	**Losses**
Prospecting						
Education and Personal Development						
Quality Time and Community Service						
Health						

Note: Consider cutting out the Scorecard tally results to carry with you for the week as a reminder on what areas to work on.

Copyright – © 2015 – John D. Mayfield, www.RealEstateSalesMeetings.com and www.RealEstateTechGuy.com

Figure 16-1 (Continued)

Epilogue

I hope that I have been able to provide some meaningful information, ideas, and strategies, or at least prompt you to think outside the box. I hope what you have learned will enable you to grow and create a successful real estate career. Most of all, I hope that you enjoy your career in real estate as much as I have treasured this profession. It truly is a dream job that I cherish, and I am so grateful to be a part of the real estate industry.

I have worked with and witnessed thousands of real estate professionals throughout my real estate tenure. I have witnessed many agents use the same information and methods discussed in this book for achieving great success in their real estate careers. Unfortunately, I have known a larger percentage of real estate professionals who chose not to use the suggested principles. These agents often ended up leaving the real estate profession early and discouraged.

As with any book or seminar you might attend, not everything will be applicable to you. There may have been some marketing strategies and ideas that made you shake your head and question whether those practices were things you could implement into your real estate practice. That's okay; the main purpose and goal of the book is to give you some concepts and tactics to help you grow your business, and it's okay if you don't use all of them.

Where do you go from here? I have provided a sample outline and suggested a plan of action for you to consider to jumpstart your career. Remember, this is not a book about how to create wealth in the next five minutes by using a few marketing campaigns. Nor is it a book about how to do something in five minutes, and immediately write a sales offer or obtain a new listing. Yes, the real estate business is like planting a garden. Planting each seed may only take five minutes, but you also have to fertilize and till the soil. Plant seeds, pull the weeds, water, and tend to your garden every day! If you follow this garden analogy, in time, you will witness a beautiful and fruitful garden!

I wish you the best of luck with your real estate career.

John D. Mayfield
Author | Broker | Speaker